BUYING · AND · SELLING
Antiques

BUYING · AND · SELLING
Antiques

A Dealer Shows How to Get Into the Business

Sara Pitzer and Don Cline

Storey Communications, Inc. Pownal, Vermont 05261

Front cover photo by Didier Delmas
Back cover photo of clock by Henry W. Art, courtesy of <u>The Library Antiques</u>,
Spring Street, Williamstown, Massachusetts.
Illustrations from "<u>A Source Book of Advertising Art,</u>" Bonanza Books, New York
and "<u>Hart Picture Archives, Volume 1, A Compendium,</u>" Hart Publishing Com-
pany, Inc., New York.
Production by Nancy Lamb and Wanda Harper
Typesetting by Quad Left Graphics, Burlington, Vermont 05451

Printed in the United States by Courier
Fifteenth printing, September 1994

Library of Congress Cataloging-in-Publication Data

Pitzer, Sara
    Buying and selling antiques

    Includes index.
    1. Secondhand trade — Handbooks, manuals, etc.
2. Selling — Antiques — Handbooks, manuals, etc.
I. Cline, Don, 1940-   II. Title.
HR5482.P57 1986   745.1'068'8   85-61478
ISBN 0-88266-407-7
ISBN 0-88266-406-9 (pbk.)

Contents

Foreword

"Here's the way to start a country antiques business."

"Oh yeah, says who?"

When anybody presumes to tell you how to do anything, you've got a right to know who they are and how they're qualified to be giving you advice. Now here we are, Don Cline and Sara Pitzer, with a whole book of advice about the antiques business. Who are we anyhow?

Don earns a living in North Carolina selling antiques from six buildings on what used to be a chicken farm. About ten years ago the cholesterol scare and low prices made producing eggs unprofitable for the Clines. Buying and selling antiques has been a way to stay on the land and still support a family. Cline's Country Antiques specializes in primitives, oak, country store items, old advertising materials, wood stoves, pottery, tools, and curios, maintaining over 15,000 square feet of constantly changing American antiques and collectibles.

Although he started small, not trying to make antiques a full-time job, today Don devotes his time solely to the antiques business and relies on help from his wife, Vikki, as well. Don sells in three different modes. Most of his business is in wholesaling by the truckload to other dealers, but he also sells pieces "as is" to individuals who come to the farm. And he refinishes some pieces to sell ready-to-use at higher prices to customers who like antiques but aren't interested in doing the refinishing work themselves.

During the ten years or so of developing his business from a part-time to a full-time operation, Don has acquired experience in every aspect of antiques dealing, from selling a few pieces at a time at flea markets to buying at high-level auctions. He's made most of the mistakes beginners in the business make. And he's seen the mistakes other people make trying to get established in antiques. Over the years he's watched lots of dealers thrive and he's seen others fail. He has helped many newcomers to the field get started in their own antiques businesses. Hearing himself repeat the same advice over and over to them, Don's often said he should write a book on how to start an antiques business.

Trouble is, Don doesn't like to write. At least not books. Knocking out "A" term papers as an agricultural economics student in graduate school and dashing off a little coffee-house-style poetry from time to time is one thing; planning a book-length project and working on it for a sustained period every day is another. When would he have time to travel to auctions, make deals to sell trucks full of furniture, talk to customers, scout flea markets and yard sales, do the paper work, and generally keep up with business? Maybe that's why bookstores aren't full of books by antiques experts on how to get into the business.

That's what Sara's good for. She's been writing how-to books for about as long as Don's been working in antiques. In the process of looking for old desks and tables and chairs to refinish for a country home in North Carolina, Sara became a repeat customer at Don's barns. As she watched him buying and selling, heard him advising customers, and asked a lot of questions herself, the notion struck her that what he knew really should be in a book.

We struck a deal — Don's expertise and Sara's writing. Beyond that, we share a preference for old things over new and an incurable penchant for teaching. *You* want to get into the antiques business. We're here to tell you how. We know you can do it and we wish you great success.

Let's get started.

CHAPTER 1

Is Antiques the Business for You?

An antiques business offers fantastic benefits to the right person. You can practice it on as large or small a scale as you please; you can immerse yourself in the antiques you love most — from oak to Oriental — jewelry to farm equipment. You can arrange your buying and selling so that you "have to" travel to sunny Florida in the winter and into the cool mountains of New England in the summer. It's an excellent occupation for retirees who'd rather sell a rocking chair than sit in it, and perhaps best of all, it's something you can do in remote areas where other kinds of jobs aren't available, because antique hunters count looking up sources hidden in the country and small towns as part of the fun of antiquing.

But check that first sentence again. We said an antiques business is great for *the right person*. Not everyone is suited to it. Indeed, not even all who love antiques are suited to getting into the business. In watching dealers come and go, Don has observed at least ten personal characteristics you need to have if you're going to be successful *and* enjoy working as an antiques dealer. Without some of these traits, you can't make it financially; without others, you can probably earn a living but you'll hate every minute of it, and working at something you hate is part of what you're trying to avoid by getting into the antiques business. As we see it, if you are interested in this business, it's partly because you are looking for a way to earn your income doing something you enjoy. Maybe you're looking for business activities that will financially justify the time, travel, and money you're already putting into the pursuit of antiques. And, surely, you're like most other people attracted to the business in wanting to work for yourself and gain more control over your life. Let's talk about what you need to be able to do to manage all this and see how you measure up.

Love antiques. You must have a passion for antiques and collectibles. Anything less than a consuming interest just won't be enough to sustain you through the long hours and inevitable frustrations and disappointments. Don spends most of the hours of most days in some activity related to the business. So do most others doing well in antiques businesses. They don't mind because it's what they'd be do-

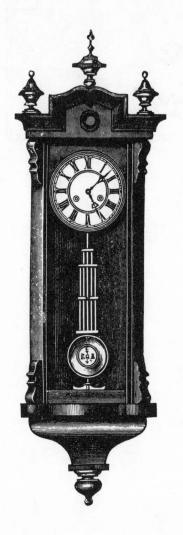

ing anyway, and, as they see it, the business allows them to indulge their passion for antiques without going broke.

A couple who liked antique clocks and bought them whenever they could soon found themselves selling one clock for money to buy a better one. Soon, people who wanted to buy old clocks began contacting the couple. So did people who wanted to sell clocks. Almost without realizing what had happened, the pair's fascination with old clocks catapulted them into a modest business specializing in buying and selling antique clocks.

A university professor bought an old player piano to fix up because he thought the activity was relaxing. He enjoyed it so much that when the first one was done, he bought another. And another. This guy had great concentration and worked steadily on any project he started until he'd finished it. How relaxing that really was is questionable, but it wasn't long before player pianos had crowded out his houseplant collection (which was doing poorly for want of attention anyhow) and his wife was pointing out that they were about two pianos away from crowding out her and the kids, too. So he sold a piano to make way for the next one and, in the process, made a nice profit. By that time, of course, the word was out. People began calling not only about buying and selling player pianos, but also about music rolls for them. The professor had already learned that you can't use a player piano without music rolls, so he'd begun collecting them, too. It takes that kind of passion to do really well in the antiques business.

Don got into the business because he was so fascinated with the old things he found at estate sales that he got into the habit of buying whole boxes and buildings full of junk. He knew he'd find a few treasures in each load. He wasn't spending as much money as you might think. A box full of junk that cost $1 sometimes turned out to have several old bottles worth $20 each; the contents of an old garage might go for $50 and have enough lumber and antique tools tucked across the beams to be worth three times as much. This brings us to a second characteristic it takes to be good in an antiques business.

Enjoy horsetrading. You need an honest-to-goodness love of horsetrading, or buying and selling. You are getting into a business where neither prices nor values are fixed and your whole aim is to buy low and sell high. Don's fondness for wheeling and dealing is nearly as great as his fascination with old things. He loves buying antiques. In her psychological analysis moments, Vikki points out that Don grew up in a family that was tight with the pennies. Don is the same way. He hates to go to malls and spend money. But, Vikki says, because buying antiques is business, that makes it "legal buying" for Don and that's why he likes it so much. He has known people who started in the antiques business with little knowledge about the antiques themselves, but with a canny knack for spotting a bargain and making a deal. One was a used car salesman before he got into antiques. When he started, it was because he enjoyed the fun of buying and selling, and he quickly became knowledgeable — an item at a time — about what he was buying and selling, just as earlier he had learned enough about automobiles to know a good car from a bad one, and to recognize a good buy when he saw one.

If you are the kind of person who is embarrassed to quote a price when someone asks you how much you want for an item or a service, think carefully before going deeply into the antiques business because unless you can get tough, you'll forever be at the mercy of people who aren't afraid to ask for what they want and who can, with impunity, try to talk you into selling your merchandise to them for less than you planned.

Decide fast. Closely related to the ability to buy and sell, a willingness to make quick decisions is essential. This, too, is related to the fact that you're always looking for the best price when you buy and the highest return when you sell. Price guides give only suggested ranges. The condition of a piece will be a factor and sometimes that's hard to tell in a hurry. And, of course, there will always be those items that come along about which you don't know enough to be sure what a good price — buying and selling — is. You can even expect times when an item shows up that you can't identify at all. But you still have to act fast or the chance to buy or sell may be gone. Making quick decisions means that sometimes you'll make mistakes, that sometimes you'll buy or sell, or fail to, and regret it later. It's part of the business. When antiques dealers get together, their running favorite conversation is swapping stories of great deals they lost, pieces they sold too cheaply, pieces for which they paid too much, and pieces they got stuck with for not selling when they could. It's a kind of black humor. The worse your goof, the better your story and the louder the collective groans. An antiques dealer who never made a mistake (if there were such a creature) probably wouldn't have much fun at such a gathering. What would there be to talk about?

Although you have to accept some mistakes, you have to develop good enough judgment so that you don't have *too* many mistakes to accept.

Here's a story of two decisions, made by two different people, about the same piece. The scene was a farm estate sale on what once had been a wealthy cotton plantation. Most of the people attending the sale were the heirs of the estate looking for pieces of sentimental value — and then there was Don. He spotted a pine corner cupboard heavily covered with red, white, and blue paint. It was sitting on a dirt floor in the back corner of an old smoke house. His first impression was that the cupboard looked "rotted, filthy, nasty, dirty." The auctioneer wasn't much interested in it and neither was anybody else. When the auctioneer asked for an opening bid of $15, Don immediately jumped it to $35 and the cupboard was his. A woman at the sale also had looked at the piece and said, "Oh, what a shame. It's too far gone. Too bad we couldn't have gotten to it before it was ruined." She didn't bother to bid.

Don loaded the cupboard into his truck, took it back to the farm, and sold it the next day to a collector for $300. That was less than ten years ago. Today, Don would give $2,500 to get it back. Obviously, his original decision to purchase the cupboard was right; the woman who passed it up because it was "ruined" was wrong. But was Don right or wrong to sell it for $300? That's $265 more than he paid for it and he didn't have it taking up space for even a day, but should he have held onto it until he could get even more? There are no absolutes here. Such buying and selling decisions are governed partly by your philosophy of doing business. (Don likes to keep merchandise moving in and out all the time.) We'll talk more about such decisions in the chapter on buying and selling. And, incidentally, you'll be hearing more about that particular estate sale, too. But now let's get back to the personal characteristics of good antiques dealers. If you understand the need for making quick decisions, you won't have any trouble understanding this next requirement either.

Accept surprises. You must be flexible enough to change your plans and to live with the unexpected. You never know when someone's going to show up to sell something you shouldn't pass up. You never know when or what customers will want to buy, either. Late one afternoon one of Don's customers showed up at his home just as he was finishing a snack. She took one look at the glass in his hand and asked if she could buy the set. He agreed. While he was getting the rest of the glasses out of the cupboard, she spotted a set of dishes and bought them, too. By the time Vikki got home, nothing was left to set the table for dinner. And, as she'd tell you, many a night when the table *was* set, someone unexpected has come driving up with a truckload of antiques to sell and the mashed potatoes and gravy have gone cold while Don exercised his love of horsetrading over a load of merchandise too good to pass up just for a warm dinner.

Your customers will want to see you when *they're* not working — weekends, holidays, and evenings. That means *your* time off is uncertain. Only a very, very well established antiques dealer can afford to say, "Go away. I don't want to see your 200-year-old pine chest because this is my day off." Officially, Don's barns are closed Sunday and Monday. He doesn't have too much trouble on Sundays, because he lives in an area where most people still take the Sabbath as a day of rest seriously. But, as Vikki says, "the idea that he doesn't work Monday is a farce." Talking about Vikki leads us directly to another concern if you're starting a business.

Hang around with saints. You need the patience and cooperation of understanding friends and family. If the people with whom you live and customarily associate are the kind who insist on predictability, punctuality, rigorously kept schedules, and making plans far in advance, you'd better give some serious thought to whether being in the antiques business is important enough to you to warrant upsetting them, possibly to the point of alienation. Some of us need more order in our lives than others. Nothing is wrong with that, but dealing in antiques is not an orderly business. We're not suggesting that being in the business gives you license to show up late for appointments, miss dinner without notice, or spend all your time away from home, but anyone who's ever started up an antiques business and made it successful will tell you that sometimes those things happen. The priorities can be tough. What's more important: getting home to dinner on time or finishing a deal that will help to pay for that dinner?

The more established you become, the more you can afford to run the business at your own convenience, but life will never become entirely predictable. What if you plan a vacation several months ahead and learn about an important sale just a couple of weeks before it's time to go? If you have kids, you're looking at a disaster. If you're a retired couple in the business together, the change will hardly ripple the waters of the lake you didn't get to when you planned.

We don't think such questions have a single right answer. We do think asking them is a good way to evaluate how well an antiques business will fit in with the rest of your life.

Your relationship with people is part of our next consideration, too.

Be social. You should like people and, ideally, be able to show it easily. Every aspect of the business, from visiting homes to appraise antiques to selling old iron skillets at flea markets puts you in contact with other people. Customers tend to look at antiques dealers a little like doctors or lawyers. They want to ask advice and tell their own stories. If you're brusque or impatient or just plain mean, you may close that sale, but the people will go to someone nicer to be around for the next deal.

In buying, you'll often encounter people selling things that have sentimental value to them — furniture or jewelry from old family homes, for example — but aren't worth as much in money as they believe. Not only is it cruel to be too blunt about it, it's stupid. Those same people may have other furniture or jewelry at home worth more than they suppose, but the only place you'll see it is in the hands of a more sympathetic dealer where they go next time.

If you are running a shop, you need as good a bedside manner as the old-time physician who dispensed more confidence than chemicals. People who come to buy antiques often are wary, not quite sure of their own judgment and not at all sure about the integrity of the people in the store. If you can make them feel confident and trusting, they'll be back.

On the other hand, as much as you like people, sometimes you have to be able to do without them.

Master solitude. You should be able to work alone. Even if you're starting a business with a spouse or partners, sometimes you'll face trips to sales or flea markets when only one of you can go. If you run a shop that you keep open regular hours, you'll have times, maybe even days, when not a single customer shows up. You'll be there alone. Refinishing furniture is usually a solitary occupation. So is doing the book work and record keeping essential to keeping your operation in the black.

Excel in business. You must have basic business skills or work with a partner who has them. Next to the ability to buy and sell, this may be the characteristic most necessary for making an antiques business profitable. When you start any kind of business, you enter a world of ledgers, laws, taxes, and records. The IRS demands a lot more punctuality and predictability from you than your friends and family. We've included the basic business information you need to start your business, including advice about how to manage employees, how to keep overhead down, and what to do about insurance. If reading these things makes you squirm with distaste, look for some help. Mastering the business details is a good way to avoid the "hobby trap."

Give up the hobby mentality. You have to learn to operate your enterprise as a business rather than a hobby, even if you started out with antiques as an avocation. Hobbyists can afford luxuries businesspeople can't: spending more on an item than it will bring on the market, walking away from it all on bad days, indulging impractical whims, giving away what could be sold, and keeping all the best merchandise for yourself, for example.

Sell what you buy. You've got to be able to avoid "keepitis." You'd be surprised at the number of people who've put themselves out of business because they like the antiques they find so much they can't sell them. If you do that, you'll end up with a beautifully furnished home — or shop, but no business.

Notice that we've said absolutely nothing about needing to be any particular size or sex or age. If you want to deal in something heavy, it would probably be helpful to be able to lift heavy things, or to have someone who will do it for you, but the antiques business has room for everybody who loves it. One of Don's favorite customers is a 96-year-old dealer who shows up every couple of months to buy a load of rough pieces. He refinishes, repairs, and resells them. He makes money. Another successful dealer didn't even start until he was past seventy. He's now in his mid-eighties and rarely misses an auction. They love what they're doing. Don does, too. He enjoys it so much that he plans to keep on doing it forever. He hopes that when he's ninety-six he'll still be buying antiques by the truckload.

If, in looking back over these characteristics, you see yourself, you're a natural for starting an antiques business. Even if you find you fall short here and there, don't give up the whole idea. Instead, try to figure out how to compensate for what (in the antiques business at least) seem to be your shortcomings. Getting into this business will be a wonderful adventure, frustrating sometimes, exhausting sometimes, even overwhelming. But the great thing about it is that you'll enjoy endless potential for development and learning. You've probably been to a class of some kind in which the program is geared to start all participants at their own level and to help them develop at their own speed. Starting an antiques business can be like that.

You don't need a lot of money, a lot of room, or even a lot of expertise about antiques to get started. You can get into it, at little risk, as deeply or as casually as you like, by starting small and growing into a business that suits you. Although we're oriented toward a country business, with lots of space available for merchandise, what we have to say applies to starting an antiques business almost anywhere. You can't sell antique farm equipment out of a third-floor efficiency apartment, but you could sell old jewelry or glass or antique miniatures from there. The basic principles would be the same. If you've decided that you're suited to the business, the next step is to decide exactly how to get it started.

CHAPTER 2
How to Get Started

Think small. Do not hurry out to rent space for a shop, fill it with antiques, get a fancy sign made, install a telephone, and start keeping regular store hours. Antiques businesses that begin this way nearly always come to a bad end — quickly. You may run out of inventory before you can get into the swing of buying. You'll probably get bored sitting around the shop waiting for customers to show up. Overhead will get way ahead of income and you'll almost certainly run out of money.

The best way to get started is to deliberately mimic some of the people who got into the business by accident.

This first story is from the young man who fixes Sara's word processor. His mother loves flea markets and knows *everything* about pink depression glass. About fifteen years ago she started entertaining herself on weekends by going to all the flea markets she could find, buying any depression glass she could find — glass mixed in with other odds and ends, often for as little as fifty cents. A sugar bowl here, a salt shaker there — she soon had boxes of the stuff crammed into her closets and filling the basement. Her husband grumbled a little about the space all the glass was taking up, but he didn't say much else because she wasn't spending a lot of money. She agreed that she didn't really *need* any more pink depression glass, but fun's fun and every Saturday she checked out as many flea markets and yard sales as she could find and kept on buying that pink glass, never spending more than a few dollars. Sometimes she sold a few pieces for money to buy a more expensive one.

Then flea markets began to change. She found whole tables full of pink depression glass, and it wasn't cheap anymore. She reversed her weekend entertainment process. Every weekend she took a few pieces of her glass *to* flea markets and sold it to those dealers who handled it and knew its increasing value. She still picked up anything she could find at a bargain price, and sometimes she traded some pieces she had in abundance for those that were harder to find. Today her collection of pink depression glass is worth about $30,000, and her buying, selling, and trading keep her inventory constantly changing. She still works almost entirely by approaching dealers at flea markets or in response to referrals. This lady is in the antiques business, making a profit. All she ever invested was her weekend time and spare pocket money.

She succeeded because she started acquiring depression glass before the rest of the buying public decided it was "collectible," and because she never stopped buying and selling. Many antiques businesses have had short lives because the would-be dealers didn't realize how hard they would have to work to maintain an inventory.

As another example, Don knows a woman who especially loves *buying* antiques. She eventually ended up, as enthusiasts usually do, with a horribly overcrowded house. She had a yard sale. The yard sale attracted so many more customers than she anticipated that she even emptied her attic. She keeps buying because that's what she loves doing, and by having several yard sales a year she manages to make some money and clear enough space to move around in her house.

Her advantages are minimal overhead and, since she's not tied to a shop, time to restock between sales. By now, customers watch for her yard-sale ads because they know she always has new pieces they haven't seen.

It was Don's love of buying that eased him into the business, too. He'd gotten into the habit of going to estate sales and auctions and buying anything he could find that was cheap. He didn't really have much sense of what he was doing, but he couldn't pass up the chances to buy whole truckloads of merchandise for $10. Regulars at the sales started calling him "Quarter Cline" because he'd give a quarter for anything. As he explains it to people these days, "If I bought it, I hauled it home." When you haul in goods a truckload at a time, the sheds fill up fast.

Other dealers and collectors started calling him offering to buy items they knew he'd picked up in one load or another. Don accepted the offers. And as he noticed that certain people asked about the same things repeatedly, he began buying with them in mind. For instance, when he saw that people wanted baskets, he'd buy baskets. When he found that he had a few regular customers, he started buying more heavily. Instead of limiting himself to $10 a load, he might spend as much as $100. Naturally, word started getting around that Don was picking up goodies; naturally, people started stopping by his house to see what he might have that they could buy. In a sense, Don didn't really choose to go into the business; it found him. On the other hand, that happened because of the buying *and selling* he was doing for fun. And, if we're going to be honest about it, his wife, Vikki, stepped up his selling activities considerably by pointing out that if he didn't start selling some of what he bought they wouldn't have anything to live on. She also said she couldn't live with people buying goods out of her house, so that she never knew what would be left when she got home at night. This led Don to keep regular business hours on the family farm, where he kept what was for sale in all the old chicken houses. At first he was open only on Sunday afternoons, because in addition to farming he had a full-time job teaching at a local college. Then he began opening on Saturday as well as Sunday because so many people wanted to shop then. Gradually, he reduced the hours he taught, and his farming activities diminished, too, because farming had ceased to be profitable. Altogether, it took about three years for Don to make the transition into antiques as a full-time business. It's important to note here that Don was not knowledgeable about antiques in the beginning and often probably didn't get what various pieces were worth, but he was nevertheless buying at a low price and selling at a higher one — a basic business practice.

To illustrate another approach to buying low and selling high, here's one more story of beginning in the business. In the course of his trading, Don met a retiree who got started because he enjoys working with his hands. First he picked up an oak washstand for $20. It didn't look like much because it had been painted several times, some of the hardware was missing, and the doors hung crooked. It took about three days for the man to strip off the accumulated layers of old paint, fix the hinges, find suitable replacement hardware, sand, and refinish the piece. It was beautiful when he was finished, but his wife didn't think it fit in with the rest of their furniture, so he loaded it into his truck and hauled it to an antique shop that specializes in ready-to-use antiques, where he sold it for about $75. It sold at retail a few days later for $125. He enjoyed himself so much, he refinished a couple more pieces and sold them at a nice markup, too. As he got more involved, he started looking for better bargains when he bought and asking market value prices when he sold. This man is in the antiques business, too. Don recommends this system for people who enjoy working on the antiques more than they do the buying and selling. The best way to go about it is to hook up with a dealer who will pay you for finished pieces and who may, also, pay you to work on pieces that come to the dealer needing attention. Some dealers will ask you to leave finished pieces on consignment. Don't do it unless it's with a person you know and trust. You wouldn't be the first person to return for your money to find the store empty and the "owner" gone.

Beginning Decisions

First, what will be the nature of your business in the early days? Let's look at the possibilities. In addition to selling at yard sales and flea markets, you can refinish and sell a piece at a time to dealers, sell on consignment in other people's shops, sell out of your home, or sell pieces in antique malls. We'll talk about each of these categories a little later. To some extent the way you begin depends partly on the kinds of antiques you're interested in or have decided to learn about. Conversely, your current living situation must govern the kinds of antiques you sell. If you live in a four-room walk-up apartment and drive a Volkswagen, you won't be able to deal in player pianos or heavy oak furniture without making some major changes

or laying out a lot of cash for storage and transportation. But you could handle old costume jewelry or dolls.

The interests and merchandise available in your area are another controlling factor for beginners. Sara collects antique miniatures (doll house furniture) and typewriters. Either would make a nice little sideline business, except for one thing. Most of the antique typewriters *and* the people interested in them are in New York City. You can find a modest collection of old typewriters here and there in North Carolina, but nowhere near enough to build a good collection, let alone start a business. No inventory supply, no potential customers — no business. The same is true of antique miniatures, except that the centers for them and the populations willing to spend money on them (they're *expensive!*) are in New England and California. Apparently, little Southern children didn't play much with doll houses, or if they did, the toys didn't survive Sherman's march. On the other hand, North Carolina is a great place to be if you're interested in primitive country furniture. The area has had many poor rural people in its history. No doubt they'd be astonished to see what the cupboards and shelves they knocked together from rough lumber sell for today.

Generally, people prefer the antiques native to their own areas. As another example, curly maple furniture is popular in the Midwest and New England states, but it was uncommon in the South and so there's little market for it there. One exception to all this is that *everything* old brings a premium price in California, because the state was settled late and old things are scarce. And if you've ever driven across the Rockies pulling even a small trailer, you understand the high cost of "imported" antiques in the state.

You can see how your location and your personal interests together will help you decide what kinds of antiques to start with.

One other factor Don considers important in deciding what merchandise to handle as a beginner is the kinds of people you will attract. Unless you are already knowledgeable about them, guns, silver, gold, coins, and expensive jewelry are bad for getting started because these items are most likely to be fake or hot, to bring you customers who write bad checks, and to appeal to shoplifters. In addition, the laws governing guns are many and variable. No dealer is allowed to sell firearms without a license, and those guns that are offered to you as a dealer are likely to leave you guilty of buying stolen merchandise. Old muzzle loaders are an exception to all this, but you can hardly make a business out of them. Moreover, if you look at the premises where firearms are the main merchandise, you find cement block buildings with steel bars reinforcing the windows. Gold, silver, good jewelry, and coins require similar protection. You don't want to live like that just to get into the antiques business! Such items also require more capital to get started. The whole idea is to start small.

Tips on Being a Small-Time Operator

How much capital does it take to start small? Surprisingly little, if you go about it Don's way. If you were to jump in all at once and try to set up a full-scale antiques shop, you'd need a minimum of $50,000, according to current wisdom. But if you begin gradually, you don't need much more than enough money to buy a single piece. The idea is to start your antiques business without giving up your other sources of income, to nurture that business into a viable concern, and then gradually to give up whatever outside jobs you may have, as Don did in reducing the number of hours he taught and farmed.

Another part of starting gradually is maintaining low overhead, no matter how or where you operate. You might be tempted to go out and buy a shiny new van and a sign to put on it, but if you *must* spend money on a vehicle, make it as inexpensive a purchase as you can and still have reliable transportation. Don does most of his hauling in a 1967 Ford 1-ton truck, with a 12-foot flat bed and rough lumber side planks, that he bought for $1,300 ten years ago. That old truck has hauled more dollars' worth of antiques than any fancy truck in the area. Similarly, Don doesn't have a separate telephone for his business. Nor does he attempt to heat his buildings, except for one room where he meets people. He doesn't pay rent on the buildings because they're part of the family property. When you're tempted to rent a building or buy an expensive truck or have fancy stationery printed, stop and figure out how much you'd have to sell each month to pay for the expenditure. That kind of thinking automatically helps you keep overhead down. As far as Don's concerned, you can't overemphasize the importance of avoiding unnecessary fixed expenses.

A related bit of advice, don't be too much of a purist in the beginning. Let's suppose you're dealing in antique clothing, for instance, and you come across an ostrich feather boa for under $1. You know it's not really old, but you also know it will appeal to some of the people who are interested in old clothing. Buy it! You'll probably be able to sell it for much more to someone trying to put together a funky look. Don't pretend that it's old; simply let your customers know that you found it, thought it was neat, and figured one of them might like it, too. Or suppose you're selling odds and ends of furniture out of your garage on weekends. One weekend you have way too many beans and tomatoes in your garden. Bag them up, put a price on them, and leave them in a conspicuous spot so your customers will know they're for sale. If you or someone in your family practices a craft — knitting or making wooden toys, for example — sell the products along with your antiques. Local folk art, handmade duck decoys, potted plants all are examples of salable objects that fit logically with antiques and will bring in a bit of money. It's a matter of orienting yourself to the notion of making a dollar. You've got customers coming; sell them *something*.

CHAPTER 3
Starting in the Business

The general principles of the preceding chapter apply in almost all situations. In this chapter, let's look more closely at some of the ways you can establish yourself in selling antiques. We'll discuss a number of different ways you can sell your merchandise. Some require a place from which to operate — your yard or garage or shop. Others allow you freedom from place because you go to the customers. You'll see advantages and problems with each possibility. Remember that no one way of selling necessarily excludes the others. If you stay in the antiques business for any length of time, you'll probably have a try at most of the activities we're describing here.

If you've accumulated some antiques, a yard sale is a good, no-risk way to find out how well you like dealing with customers and whether you have merchandise that will sell in your area.

Your sale will differ from standard yard sales in that you'll be offering mostly antiques, not raggedy baby clothes and jigsaw puzzles with missing pieces. To attract the right customers, you'll need to advertise. An ad in the "yard sale" category of the newspaper classifieds will be fine because antique hunters watch such ads. Just make sure your ad clearly states that you're offering antiques. It's a good idea to mention specifically a couple of desirable pieces. And if your location is especially remote, be sure to include simple directions for finding your place. You can try to work up something more eye-catching if you're good at that sort of thing, but it really isn't necessary. In the end, it will probably make your advertisement longer and more costly. If you're offering good antiques, something direct and simple like our samples will do fine.

In preparing for your sale, it is critical that you look around to see what comparable merchandise is bringing in good shops, then set your prices in that range, leaving a little room to come down for customers who think that haggling is a fun part of the whole yard sale scene. People tend either to have an overinflated idea of what their merchandise is worth or to undervalue it. A couple who lived next to Sara's parents in Sequim, Washington, illustrate both extremes. Their house was bulging with many years' accumulation of antiques, furs, good china, and even jewelry. When they decided to

Yard Sales

have a yard sale, Vic suggested prices for everything. Martha said they were all too high and made him put much lower stickers on their goods. But after Martha went to bed, Vic went around and raised most of the prices. Martha never knew because she had bad eyesight and Vic handled the actual selling. They got Vic's price on practically everything — which suggests that it never hurts to try. But if interested people had turned away after looking at the prices, Vic would've had to lower them again. The example shows you just how hard it is to find the line between undervaluing and overvaluing what you have. Often people who've had antiques for a long time and decide to sell them don't charge enough because they haven't kept track of the market. But almost anybody will tend to ask too much for a piece that has sentimental value or a history of family stories attached to it.

If you have some choice pieces on which you want the highest possible return, you can use a make-an-offer sticker, and mentally fix a minimum price you'll accept.

After you've priced everything, make up an inventory list with the prices. Don't forget to include the lowest acceptable price on any make-an-offer items. As you sell the items, cross them off the list, making sure you note any prices you've changed for hagglers.

As always, in the interest of bringing in money however you can, it's perfectly okay to include nonantiques in your yard sale, but avoid old shoes and broken crock pots and anything else you know perfectly well is worthless. They'll just waste your energy and turn off your customers. Also, resist the impulse to put out a few clothes you'd like to get rid of, because many antique hunters who drive around scouting the yard sales won't stop at places where they see piles and racks of clothes. (Antique clothes are an exception.) You're trying to convey the sense of offering quality bargains — not junk.

Try to have at least one reliable helper who can take money, keep track of the inventory list, and help get sold pieces out of the yard, so that you can talk to customers and answer their questions without losing sales.

Let customers know that you plan more sales if the first one is successful. Tell them to watch for your ads and give them an idea of when to expect the next sale.

Selling antiques at a yard sale has almost no disadvantages except for a couple of days' inconvenience (getting ready is a lot of work, and smart shoppers *always* show up early and form a little crowd in the yard the day of the sale). In most places you don't have to get any kind of permit to have a yard sale, although some areas limit the number of sales you may hold in a given period of time; you don't have to worry about hauling the pieces anywhere; and once it's over your place goes back to normal. If your supply of antiques is modest, say only as many as you can buy and refinish yourself, the yard sale could be your best and most profitable outlet for a long time.

But, if you get restless and want to move around, if you'd like to see what other people are selling, if you're looking for more new customers, or if you're dealing in a narrow area of specialization with only a limited local market, you might try flea markets.

Flea Markets

Going to flea markets can introduce you to the business and be lots of fun. It gets you into the camaraderie of the antiques-selling crowd, gives you a chance to see what people are paying for various kinds of merchandise, and gives you experience buying and selling. It's also lots of work. Unless you live in an unusual area, you'll probably have to drive some distance to find a flea market big enough to bother with. If you're just selling odds and ends, not good antiques, or if you're looking for some experience before you hit the serious flea markets, you may be able to accomplish all you want at a local charity-sponsored sale, but if you're serious about using flea markets as a way into the antiques business, you'll have to do more. Don strongly recommends finding the largest flea market in your area, one that attracts people from several communities, and starting there.

Since you're interested in antiques, you probably already have a good idea about where to find such flea markets. In addition, consult the classified advertisements in newspapers and the listings in *The Antique Trader Weekly,* as well as any other antiques-related publications you read. (We'll mention *The Antique Trader Weekly* more than once in this book. It's the one publication that's almost essential to your knowing what goes on in the business. The address is: *The Antique Trader Weekly,* Box 1050, Dubuque, Iowa 52001.) You can almost certainly find not only *The Antique Trader Weekly* but lots of smaller, regional publications with more local news by asking an established dealer about periodicals. In our area, for instance, *The Mid Atlantic Antique & Auction Magazine* (P.O. Box 908, Henderson, North Carolina 27536) and *Carolina Antique News* (P.O. Box 241114, Charlotte, North Carolina 28224) are two inexpensive tabloid-style publications with news and advertising about flea markets, auctions, current tastes, important personalities, and shops. Every part of the country has comparable papers. We have listed as many as possible beginning on page 92, but you will almost certainly find others we don't know about in your area. These are essentially trade journals, sometimes slanted toward both dealers and buyers. You should subscribe to them. They'll be especially useful to you in finding flea markets, but you'll find their information part of keeping up with current developments in the antiques business. They contain ads for forthcoming auctions and also stories written by their reporters about results and prices at recent auctions. This is information you need even if you eventually stop going to flea markets entirely.

But let's not talk about stopping until we've gone into more detail about getting in to begin with. It's better to reserve your space ahead of time than to simply show up with a load of merchandise and hope you'll be able to unload it someplace. Usually, the best spots go to "regulars," people who contract in advance to show up (and pay) for a specific number of shows. For instance, if the market is open twelve times a year, the choice locations would go to the dealers who sign up for all twelve shows. Some flea markets are open several days a week, every week. In those situations you'd contract for an agreed-upon number of dates. But it's also possible to rent space as you go, and this is probably better for you until you see how you do at any given flea market. Except for such obvious things as being inside when the weather is terrible, location is not as important when you're selling antiques as it would be in some other situations, because antique hunters also become regulars — canny about spotting new blood and bargains wherever they're located.

The number of flea markets you attend depends partly on how much you have to sell. Don't go if you don't have enough. This sounds simplistic, but Don knows several people he calls "antique groupies," who have so much fun at flea markets that they go even when they don't have enough merchandise to sell to cover the cost of the trip. If all you want is a working vacation, that's okay; if you're serious about being in business, it's a wrong move.

You're especially likely to sell out too fast if your antiques are underpriced. Beginners, especially those who have collected their antiques over a period of time, often price them in line with what they recall having bought them for, and if the goods have accrued in value at a normal rate for antiques, that price probably will be too low. That's why before you sell anything anywhere you should spend time looking around other antique shops and flea markets to get a sense of the current market. If you find that when you show up at flea markets, dealers buy everything you have before you even get set up, start raising your prices until the activity levels off — unless you don't really want to be there and are in a hurry to get out of the sun!

The problems of pricing are complicated further by the fact that prices on the same items will vary from place to place. Looking, listening, and experience are the only ways to learn pricing. We will discuss it in greater detail in the following chapters. For now, it's enough to say that if you get to a flea market and sense that the prices you intended to charge are too low (or for that matter, too high), change them. Flea market customers like to haggle, too, so that old saying applies: the selling price is whatever price a buyer and a seller agree on.

A couple more advantages to working flea markets are that you can become known quickly through the regular exposure, and that you can learn a lot about the business from spending time with more experienced dealers and collectors. As your particular specialties become known, customers will send you more customers. Other dealers will send you people who want to sell items that fit especially in your line. You'll definitely want to take a generous supply of business cards to pass out freely when you start going to flea markets. The cards don't have to be fancy or expensive. They should contain your name and the name of your busines (if the two are different), along with a phone number and address and as much explanation of your special areas of dealing as will fit attractively on the card. They can range from simple cards cut up and stamped at home to elaborately designed and printed cards. We think your card should reflect the kind of business you run. A cute or fancy card would be silly and confuse potential customers if you sell antique farm equipment or crude primitive antiques, but a cute card might be appropriate if you specialize in toys, and a fancy one would be almost mandatory if your area was fine silver or expensive Oriental furniture. Put some thought into the card's design and be sure the print is large enough for people to read all the information easily. You'll be surprised at the number of calls, letters, and referrals that seem to be inspired by passing out your business card when you're at flea markets.

If flea markets are such a great place to do business, do you wonder why everybody doesn't go? Actually, when you attend some of the larger two- and three-day flea markets, you'll have the sensation that everybody *is* there, but it's a fact that some people never go and others who used to go haven't sold that way in years — including Don. Don's reason for avoiding flea markets is simple. He hates and despises all that loading and unloading, packing everything into the truck, hauling it someplace, pulling it all out of the truck and arranging it in a space, sitting with it a day or two, then wrestling the leftovers back into the truck to haul them home where you have to drag them *out* of the truck again and back into storage buildings. But don't forget, Don handles a lot of oak and pine furniture, big old dressers and pie safes, and sometimes old woodburning stoves. Maybe he'd feel differently if his line was mostly pocket watches, postcards, and cameras. Of course, the packing would still use up a lot of time — a commodity in short supply for Don.

When time matters, some people resort to the opposite extreme of flea markets — selling in antique malls.

Antique Malls

Don's view is that antique malls are for people too proud to sell at flea markets. You've probably shopped in antique malls yourself, especially if you've browsed in large tourist areas where, as Don puts it, people are especially desirous of being separated from their money. Antique malls rent spaces for dealers to display merchandise and provide someone to wait on customers, so that your pieces are available in a shop-like situation without your having to be there tending the shop. Usually such malls charge a monthly rent of anywhere from $50 to $100, plus a commission of anywhere from 10 to 20 percent on anything they sell for you. Unless you can find a mall that charges no commission, you're going to have a hard time making money this way. Some dealers rent booths at malls in several different good market areas, especially resort areas, and then tour the circuit, visiting each booth periodically to check the display, restore the inventory, and collect the money. What makes their trips worthwhile is that, at the same time, they look for bargains in other shops in each locality. Another problem, in addition to the cost of being in the mall, is that you must keep your space filled, because you'll be paying for it whether you have anything much to sell in it or not. But even though you're going to have a fairly large amount of money tied up in your mall display, you can't count on big sales, because you can't count on the people who work in such malls to work as hard at selling your antiques as you would yourself. It you want to sell high-ticket items and can locate a mall with other expensive merchandise and a lot of customers who can afford it, you might do well in a mall in the long run. Otherwise, unless you can find a mall that charges a very low monthly rate and little or no commission, this probably isn't the best place for beginners. You'll do better to start on a smaller scale, selling out of your home first.

Selling from Home

If you do this by appointment, on a modest scale, without putting out a sign, you probably won't have to worry about any permits or licenses, even if you live in an area zoned residential. A call to your local courthouse will tell. Some people sell antiques this way for years. In the trade they are sometimes called "attic dealers." The advantages are minimal overhead and the ability to arrange your schedule to your convenience. The disadvantages are some loss of privacy because you have to let people (possibly strangers) into your home, and the loss of some impulse or walk-in customers.

We know a fascinating example of this approach. A couple in Charlotte, North Carolina, have furnished their entire home with Victorian antiques — and everything in it is for sale, by appointment only. They don't spend any time at all browsing for antiques. They buy now only to replace what they sell. Suppose, for instance, they sell a Victorian sideboard from their dining room. They'll call dealers they known in rural areas and put out the word that they need another Victorian sideboard. Most people don't do it quite this way, but for this couple — and their customers — it works.

To sell antiques out of your own home, about all you need, besides the antiques, is a way of letting the right people know what you have to sell. Word-of-mouth is unquestionably the best way of getting the information out, but small classified ads work, too. It's a good idea to get a telephone answering machine so you can respond to any inquiries that come in while you're out.

In the interests of safety and sanity, try to find some way to separate your selling space from your actual living quarters. A separate room or attached garage with an outside entrance will work.

If you have unused buildings on the property, use them. You could even have someone build a simple shed or pole barn at a very low cost. Any building you can lock, that will keep your antiques protected from the weather, will do — an old shed, garage, barn, or, as in Don's case, chicken house. That's why starting a *country* antiques business can be such a good idea. Almost all rural property has on it a couple of unused outbuildings. Customers don't expect such setups to be arranged like fancy shops. In fact, most of them consider rummaging around in the junk part of the fun. Don believes some customers are suspicious of elaborately arranged and carefully dusted displays. They think that if you have time to do all that you must not be doing much business. Nor do customers expect such buildings to be heated in winter or cooled in summer, although if you begin spending a significant amount of time in the building, you'll probably want to put in a wood or coal stove for your own comfort.

In the beginning, Don recommends that you work mostly by appointment. You can experiment with being open to all comers on Saturdays to build up business. As your business increases, you can increase the number of days you're open without appointments, as Don did.

You can get into the antiques business in one other way that lets you begin on a small scale by selling just a piece or two at a time.

Selling Pieces One at a Time

If you want to build up your business with almost no initial investment, letting it grow entirely from its own proceeds, this is a good way to begin. You buy and refinish a piece and then sell it to a dealer for resale. Some dealers will suggest taking pieces on consignment, but unless you are working with a good and trusted friend, consignment is not a good idea. For one thing, if the piece is going to sell, a good dealer will want to buy it. The other point is that there's always the risk of losing both your antique and your money to an unstable or dishonest dealer. If you know a dealer *very* well, consignment may be safe enough, but you still don't have the use of your money while the piece sits in the shop. An outright sale is better.

If your interest is in antiques that don't need refinishing or fixing, you may just do a little cleaning to make them look ready-to-use. For instance, the antique glassware and silver you see in resort hotel gift shops is always sparkling and expensive. A shiny polished glass and silver pitcher will certainly cost a lot more than the same pitcher would if you found it encrusted with mud and bird droppings in a dusty box full of old dishes back in the corner of a shed somewhere.

Many people can and will pay the extra price for getting such a piece the easy way, by selecting it from a nicely arranged display shelf in a gift shop. Your profit comes from finding the piece and getting it ready for that display.

If these kinds of arrangements appeal to you, just make the rounds of appropriate shops, talk to the owners, and make the best deals you can. You can have such a connection with one dealer or several, depending on how hard you want to work, and your corresponding ability to keep them supplied. Remember as you negotiate that even though the shop owners are helping you by providing an outlet for your antiques, you also are helping them by providing quality merchandise for their shops. Don't be so grateful that you give away too much. You're in the business to make money, just as they are. On the other hand, realize that your price on a piece must allow for the dealer's markup without running the final retail price so high that no one will pay it. The whole idea, for you and your dealers, is to keep that merchandise moving.

Finally, if fixing, refinishing, and cleaning old things seems too much like work because all you really want to do is look for antiques, maybe you can be a "picker" or "door knocker."

Picking and Door Knocking

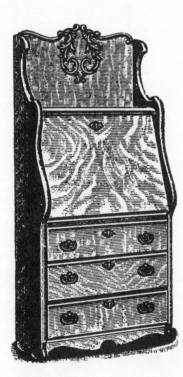

You can guess from the names what pickers and door knockers do. It's not for everyone. To put it simply, you can make a profit by finding and buying antiques at a low price and selling them, as is, somewhere else at a higher price. Sometimes this is mostly a matter of location. For example, we could pick up an old chair or desk from almost any antiques barn in rural North Carolina, take it to the city of Charlotte, where the greater population means a bigger market and hence more demand, and sell it to a dealer there at a profit. He will be able to resell it for more simply because he has access to a bigger market.

But serious door knocking involves more. Door knockers and pickers look for antiques not only at yard sales and in old sheds full of junk, but also they really do go as far as knocking on the doors of people's homes and asking if they've got any old furniture to sell. They usually concentrate on the houses in older neighborhoods. You often find people with old tables, chairs, cupboards, and sideboards that they've used for years and that their parents used before them. Such pieces have sometimes been covered with many layers of paint.

The problem here is that the owner has no idea of the value of his pie safe and pine table. His view of it is that he's being offered $65 for some old junk he's had around forever. The picker knows the pie safe will retail for more than $300 and the table is worth more than $100. Of course, *he* won't get that much if he sells it to a dealer for resale, but he'll still get substantially more than he has paid for the pieces. Is it ethical to take advantage of the owner's ignorance?

Don has made it a point to pay a fair wholesale price when he finds himself in such situations, but door knockers usually don't. The situation is not as black and white as it looks. Strangely enough, sometimes telling the owner what the wholesale value of his pieces is scares him and he won't sell at all. He still thinks the stuff is junk, but now he knows somebody else believes it to be worth money and he's afraid of making a mistake. When that happens, everybody loses. The antiques continue to languish unappreciated under layers of paint and piles of canning jars. The owner doesn't get any money; the dealer doesn't get any antiques.

To complicate things more, think of it this way. Suppose a door knocker is driving along a back road and spies a shed full of old furniture. As he pulls into the driveway, he can tell that there are at least two really rare old pieces in that shed. He can tell they are going to need work to be salable, but because they are in demand and hard to find, he knows they will bring top dollar. He knocks on the door of the house and is answered by an elderly widow who says she doesn't know and doesn't care what is in that shed. It was all just a lot of trash her husband kept around. If he wants to clean out the shed and haul everything away, he can have the contents for $50.

What are the door knocker's obligations? What's right? If he hauls everything away, sells the good pieces, and makes a profit, is he taking money from the hands of an elderly widow? She clearly won't do anything with the merchandise on her own. She probably wouldn't understand if he tried to explain the value of a couple of pieces of broken furniture to her. Hasn't he really done her a favor by clearing out her shed and hauling the junk away and paying her $50 she wasn't expecting besides?

In the antiques business, nearly everybody simply accepts the finders-keepers view of picking. They put the question of how wrong it is to gain by taking advantage of another person's ignorance aside, partly because no matter how sophisticated they are, inevitably *they* end up being the "ignorant" person who loses money from time to time. Win a few, lose a few. It's that kind of business. An additional salve to the conscience is that the picker is performing a service and he deserves to be paid for it. Without his eye and initiative, the goods wouldn't get into the marketplace at all.

Sometimes very wealthy neighborhoods yield surprising goods. For instance, there's the time two young door knockers from whom Don often buys antiques were driving through one of the most expensive neighborhoods in Charlotte, North Carolina. One of them spotted what can only be described as the mansion of all mansions and said, "Hey, let's stop there."

"You've got to be kidding," the other boy replied.

"Ah, come on. Who knows, they might have some old stuff they'd like to get rid of."

"Can't hurt. Why not?"

In a mood of adventure and devil-may-care fun, they knocked on the door and asked their question. The woman who answered the

door said, "You're the answer to my prayer. My son from Cleveland was here last week, and he says all that clutter I've got in the attic is a fire hazard and I should clear it out."

The kids could hardly wait to get the truck filled and get back to Don's farm to sell their treasures and tell their story. The load brought them several thousand dollars.

In addition to actually knocking on doors at random, door knockers drive around checking the accumulated odds and ends in open sheds and *then* knocking on the door to make an offer on something they see.

In well-to-do neighborhoods, they drive around on trash collection days, before the trucks get there, to pick up some surprisingly valuable discarded odds and ends at the curb. (One of Don's regular customers, who can afford anything she wants, scouts her own neighborhood this way and has sold many such "found" pieces. The last time he saw her, she was hauling not only antiques but also some discarded ironwork she was taking to sell at a junkyard. Don admires her pleasure in turning an extra dollar wherever she can — even though she doesn't need to.)

Another way door knockers get into a house is by answering classified "for sale" ads. One might spot an ad offering an old wood-burning cookstove for $50, for instance. In checking either the address or, more likely, the phone number, the picker determines that the stove is in an old, isolated house in the country. He'll make an appointment to look at the stove. Once inside, he'll look around to see what else in the house might be worth buying. The conversation might sound like this:

Door knocker: "Well, I don't think I want to put $50 into a woodstove right now, but I'll give you $50 for that pie safe over in the corner."

Owner: "Oh, I dunno. I hadn't even thought about selling that. I don't know where I'd put all the stuff I got in there."

Door knocker: "Let me see it. Maybe I could buy the contents, too. I'd kind of like to have that pie safe. And while I'm hauling it off, I'll give you $15 more for that old pine table holding canning jars in the pantry."

Owner: "That old thing? My mama and daddy was eatin' at that table before I was even born. I guess I could put those jars somewhere else."

Everybody has to work out the answer to such questions for himself. Don avoids it as much as he can by not getting himself into such places to begin with, although he does buy regularly from door knockers who have had to think about such questions.

In addition to such ethical questions, there is the reality that door knockers can't afford to pay regular wholesale value on what they find. Even in unpicked areas, they may drive around for several days without finding *anything*. Then they may hit several good places in a row, but the money they make has to cover the cost of their time and gas for the fallow days as well. This means they have to buy what they find cheaply or it isn't worth bothering.

A final consideration in door knocking is the danger of being considered a flim-flam artist if you're working areas where you're not known. A door knocker stopped at a property where he saw an old house falling apart behind the current residence. An 80-year-old man and his son-in-law said they would be delighted to sell the furniture in the unoccupied house. Money changed hands and the furniture was hauled away. When the elderly man's daughter got home, she called the sheriff and said her father had been cheated. The sheriff impounded the furniture, and the case went to trial before a local judge. The woman claimed that both her father *and* her husband were incompetent and had been cheated out of a fair price for the furniture.

The picker was locked up in the local jail, scared to death. The case was finally settled out of court. The woman agreed to drop the charges provided she got the furniture back. The picker didn't get his money back.

Picking Shops

Here's a safer kind of picking, especially suited to people who travel a lot for another job or just for fun. To be successful, you must have a specialty and be knowledgeable about it. Then you visit the shops wherever you go, looking for items in your specialty. When you find them cheap, you buy them and sell them at a higher price to other shops. The reason it works is because shops usually have a few specialties and their operators are often not particularly knowledgeable about or interested in objects outside those specialties. Suppose, for example, that your specialty is antique buttons. An astonishing number of people collect antique buttons. Good ones are increasingly hard to find. Your business takes you to Stroudsburg, Pennsylvania; Manchester, New York; and Williamstown, Massachusetts. In each place, you visit shops where no one much cares about antique buttons. They're cheap. You buy them. And then you start hitting the shops that cater to button collectors! If you had another specialty besides buttons — say postcards or clocks — you could watch for more goodies and sell to more shops.

Shop pickers specialize in everything from wicker to military memorabilia and Barbie dolls. This is a great way to ease into the business without giving up your other job while you build up your expertise, cash reserves, and contacts.

Looking at the ways you can get into the business points up one of the factors that makes antiques fun, sometimes risky, and always uncertain. Since the value of everything depends on who wants it and how badly, you will never be able to count on any buying or selling prices being firmly and permanently established. That's the challenge of the business. In the next two chapters we'll try to give you some additional insights into buying and selling successfully.

CHAPTER 4
All About Auctions

You can attend a variety of different kinds of auctions, ranging from the fine, top-level auctions held by such prestigious houses as Sotheby Parke Bernet, Inc., to the boisterous Coke-and-hotdog country auctions where everyone stands around in the muddy yard of an old farmhouse. Except for matters of costume and decorum, what you do at one is pretty much the same as what you do at another. Let's consider the different categories into which you can divide auctions.

Auction houses. Mid- and top-level auctions, held by Sotheby's and Christies and many less famous auction houses, are usually in cities and usually specialize in fine furniture, art, and jewelry. Such auctions are conducted in well-appointed rooms where most of the clientele is well dressed and looks wealthy and aristocratic. These sales attract art dealers, museum curators, and people with lots of money to spend. It's easy to be intimidated by such an atmosphere if you're not accustomed to it, but don't avoid such auctions on the theory that you can't afford anything there. The 1984–1985 issue of the Better Homes and Gardens publication *Traditional Home* reported that 60 percent of the items sold by Sotheby's to date have cost their purchasers under $500. And at the less ritzy mid-level auctions, prices often are under $300. (Prices are sometimes higher than *that* at country auctions held out behind the barn.) You may be able to pick up a piece that seems out of place to other bidders at a bargain price.

Don can trace the story of a pie safe to illustrate the point. He bought an unusually large pie safe from a door knocker for $100. The next day he sold it for $250 to an out-of-town dealer. Six months later he was at a fancy auction where fine, expensive items were bringing prices he'd never imagined possible. After selling a number of those expensive and polished pieces, the auctioneer turned to a load of rough country items: corner cupboards, pine tables — and Don's pie safe. It had been refinished, but poorly. Compared to the fine furniture that had been selling, it looked as dowdy as workboots on a ballerina. Don bought it back with an opening bid of $50. Immediately after the auction, Don sold the pie safe, *again*, off the back of his old farm truck for $300. He was glad to lighten his load a bit, because

Auctions Are Not All the Same

during the course of the auction he had bought almost all the other rough country pieces that had been offered. He got the load for about 20 percent of what the same goods would have cost him at an estate sale.

Estate auctions. The less elegant term is "dead man's sale." We'll use it here because it gets so directly to why you need to beware of sales disposing of the goods of people who've died, especially prominent people. People will pay more for pieces at a dead man's sale than they would pay for the same piece, refinished, in a shop. Why? Everything tends to sell at inflated values for several reasons. First, the heirs of the estate often bid against each other at these sales for pieces to which they attach sentimental value: "I just have to have Aunt Lizzie's chair. That's where I always sat while she was teaching me to crochet." Don once saw an antique sewing machine not worth more than $50 sell for $1,000. Even if you don't buy anything, this can be dangerous for you as a beginner because you'll tend to suppose the prices you're observing are standard. It will distort your sense of what similar pieces are worth on the market. The heirs may try to influence the sale by bidding up prices to protect the value of the estate, too. If the dead person was a celebrity, lots of people who aren't even related are going to show up and pay too much for what's being sold just so they can say they own something that used to belong to a famous person. And a final complication at such sales is that auctioneers sometimes bring in their own merchandise to "pack the sale," because they know it will be a good place to sell to less discriminating buyers. Often, auctioneers also bring glassware and other items that are neither valuable nor old. As you gain experience, you will be able to identify these situations and stay out of trouble, but until you've learned to recognize the real value of antiques, don't do a lot of buying at dead man's sales.

Antique auctions. These are sometimes called "country auctions" or "dealer auctions" depending on where in the country you live. They are what most of us think of when we hear about antique auctions. Usually they are held in a local auction house, sometimes outside. Often the publicity for these auctions advertises antiques hauled in from out of state. If you're in Pennsylvania, some of the antiques will be advertised from New York; if you're in New York, they'll be from Pennsylvania. In North Carolina, antiques often are hauled in from Pennsylvania. These auctions are entertainment for some people and serious work for many others. You can find everything from spectacular bargains to pure junk at these sales. Your caution here, as a buyer, is that when you're surrounded by junk, a piece that is only slightly better — let's say pretty good — looks better than it really is. And in that situation, some merely pretty good pieces will probably bring more than they are worth. That's nice if you're selling but important to avoid when you're buying.

However, we definitely are not suggesting that all you can find is junk and "pretty good pieces." A tremendous amount of merchandise turns over at these auctions, including some excellent pieces and some outstanding bargains. If you are interested in primitives, country-look, old oak, implements, and cast iron, you're more likely to find them at country auctions than anywhere else. These sales are where you go to buy boxes of junk that yield goodies, where you can sometimes pick up the contents of a trunk along with the trunk itself, and where sometimes you make a truly priceless find because nobody else, including the auctioneer, knows its true value. At country auctions, especially in the South, the auctioneers may actually be *cattle* auctioneers. They don't much like or care about antiques, but nobody else around knows how to run an auction, so they do the job.

A variation on the standard antiques auction is the one-shot auction, sometimes held for charity, sponsored by a women's club or other organization. Since the people running these don't expect to hold over any merchandise until another sale, and since the clientele aren't often professionals, you occasionally will find good buys cheaper than you would at other kinds of auctions. Of course, you'll probably have to wait through a lot of junk before you come to what you want, and your time is a value to consider, too.

Moving and storage warehouse sales. When someone stores goods and then fails to pay to reclaim them, the company that stored them often is allowed to have a sale to settle the storage bill. The sales are usually held in a dusty, overcrowded warehouse where it's too hot for comfort and hard to move around. They are not fun. That's why Don loves them. It's possible to find outstanding merchandise — good furniture and fine paintings, for instance — and no Saturday afternoon crowd is entertaining itself bidding up prices. The warehouse people are pleased to get rid of the unclaimed goods and just want to get their money. They have no emotional attachment to what they're selling that would inflate the prices they expect. Serious buyers who are willing to sweat and get dirty can find bargains at moving and storage warehouse sales.

Bankruptcy and tax sales. You may feel a little sad thinking about these sales until you realize that for the banks and the government they are a last resort. No one who is seriously trying to work out financial problems with the people in question is apt to be subjected to a bankruptcy sale. Don likes to buy at these because typically no one involved has any interest at all in the merchandise beyond getting rid of it. If the owner should be present, he perversely hopes the stuff will bring next to nothing. This means your chances are good of picking up some pieces with high resale value for very little.

Dealer's going-out-of-business sales. People avoid these sales because they assume no dealer will sell the good things. Don has found quite the opposite to be true. Often a dealer is going out of business because he or she has fallen on hard times and is desperate. Because so few knowledgeable people show up at the sale, the poor dealer may not get anywhere near what the pieces could bring. If the dealer were *dead,* Don observes, everything would go for a fortune!

Junk auctions. The name says it. These are the sales of general merchandise, sort of a mixture of garage clean-outs and bad yard sales that are typically held every Friday or Saturday night somewhere local. The auctioneer sells whatever individuals bring in to sell. Somebody always brings Taiwan tools and plastic flowers and sets of cracked dishes. Sara used to go to the Thursday night sale sometimes in Millheim, Pennsylvania, and the only thing she ever bought was a yellow teapot for fifty cents. Other people from the neighborhood who went tended to buy odds and ends to furnish their hunting camps.

Sometimes, by mistake, a good antique gets into the mix. The best walnut chest in Don's home was found by one of his pickers for $50 at a Saturday night junk sale. If no better sales are going on, check the junk sales, but don't be surprised if you get too bored to stay long.

Those are the basic kinds of auctions you're apt to attend. As we said, what you actually do at them is much the same no matter which kind it is. In the following several pages, we will look at the general principles of how to begin buying at auctions. And this seems like an appropriate place to say a word or two about auctioneers, because much of what we say involves auctioneers' actions, reasoning, and tricks of the trade. Some of it will sound questionable as far as fairness and honesty go. Having attended at least one auction a week for the past ten years, Don concludes that auctioneers are no more dishonest than the rest of us, it's just that what some of them consider proper differs from what the general public thinks proper. Approaching an antiques business with the view that the auctioneer is the enemy doesn't make any more sense than going into publishing if you don't like either writers or book buyers. If you understand the things that auctioneers do and why they do them, you can establish some mutually rewarding relationships with them in perfect honesty, and see your business improve as a result.

In the following pages we will talk about how to act at an auction, how to demystify bidding, and how to get through an auction without putting yourself near bankruptcy.

How to Act at Auctions

You can read an awful lot of garbage about how to buy at auctions, much of it having to do with feinting and faking, including: spending huge amounts of money at the beginning of an auction, whether you want what's being offered or not, to intimidate other buyers;

standing at the back of the room so no one can see that you are bidding; pointing out flaws in the antiques to discourage other bidders; and arranging special signals with the auctioneer. It is true that in certain high-powered auctions, when thousands and perhaps even hundreds of thousands of dollars are at stake and where the pieces being auctioned are uncommonly rare or desirable, the pros have used various psychological ploys to gain advantage over each other. But for most of us in the business, most of the time, buying at auction is simple and straightforward. Anybody who goes to a country auction or estate sale and buys everything offered in the beginning will end up broke, with a lot of unsalable junk and perhaps a few overpriced good things to haul home. If you stand at the back of a room in a country auction house, you'll have trouble bidding at all because people will keep getting in your way as they go to buy Cokes and popcorn. Pointing out flaws in an antique will make people wonder why you want it so badly. And the only signal an auctioneer needs is a clear, quick sign that you will pay the price. His job is simply to sell the goods at the highest price possible. This is true in an auction house, at an estate sale, and at a bankruptcy sale. An auctioneer's reputation is made partly by his ability to get top dollar for what he sells. Intrigue isn't really part of it, although there are tricks to the trade.

First, we'll give you five basic things you should do at *every* auction where you hope to buy, then we'll tell you more about how auctioneers work and why, because we think this will help you evaluate what you see and hear at auctions.

When you go to an auction, *always:* 1) arrive early; 2) look over everything and then look closely at everything you have even a remote chance of buying; 3) set mental limits on what you will pay for the pieces you're interested in (if you're easily caught up in the excitement of bidding, write down your limits where you can see them); 4) find a seat right up front, where the auctioneer can see you and you can see what he is offering; 5) when you want to bid, do it quickly and clearly.

Arriving early at an auction gives you time to look over everything generally and think about what you want. It assures you of getting a good seat and gives you time to ask questions. More important, it gives you time to *look hard* at the pieces you want to buy. This is especially important at dealer or country auctions where much of what is being offered is probably there because dealers couldn't sell it in their shops. We can scarcely overemphasize the importance in auction situations of examining what you want to buy in minute detail, because once you buy it, it's yours. No matter what you find wrong with it, you own it.

Don is keeping a huge, beautiful pine corner cupboard in one of his sheds for a friend who bought it, without inspecting it, at an auction. It's so nice looking that when you see it your first reaction is to wonder whether you have any room where it would fit in your house. Don's friend is the kind of dealer who is especially knowledgeable about fine antiques. He's been known to buy an entire houseful of junk to get one or two superior pieces, knowing he can sell the junk wholesale and not lose money on it. In short, he is a careful buyer. But on the night he bought the corner cupboard, he arrived late and came in the back door just as the bidding started on the corner cupboard. He was too far back to see that it had round nails and new hardware, which is important because round nails don't go back any further than about 1920. He asked the auctioneer, "Is it old?" Unwritten auction code demands an honest answer to this question. The auctioneer said, "Yes. It's old. It's good." This meant the piece was considered a genuine antique. That was good enough for Don's friend. He bid and hit at $750, but he had made a terrible mistake.

And when he got the beautiful, old antique pine corner cupboard home and looked at it closely, he saw that it had been built by someone's ancestor for a specific crooked corner in a specific house. The back was specifically crooked and that corner cupboard would never fit into any other corner, unless perhaps someone had a house built to fit the cupboard. Worse yet, the peculiar shape of the back affected the shelves so that it was impossible to display dishes on them in the normal way. The piece is unsalable. Had he looked at it ahead of time, he would never have bid on it.

The day we were discussing this part of the book, Don repeated at least a dozen times that we had to stress and restress the importance of looking closely at anything before bidding on it. The next day we were talking on the phone. Near the end of our conversation, he paused and then said, "We've *really* got to stress that point about inspecting what you buy." Sara said okay and before she'd even picked up a pencil, Don said he had been at an auction the night before and paid top dollar for an oak secretary that, when he went to load, he discovered had no interior and no shelves.

All the usual how-could-you's and why-didn't-you-follow-your-own-advice's seemed inappropriate, but Don explained anyway. He hadn't looked at the secretary because he hadn't expected to bid on it, supposing it would bring more than he planned to spend on any one piece there. When the bidding started low, it caught him by surprise and he made a bid. In his words, "I got in and I was on the money and the next thing I knew, I owned it." It's a rare auction where you can change your mind later. What you see is what you get and after you get it, you got it. In this case, the reason the bidding started low was probably because all the buyers who *had* looked at the secretary knew it had no interior or shelves.

With Don in this humble mood, Vikki thought we should include "The African Totem Pole Story," to reinforce the lesson and, incidentally, to demonstrate how easily even experts can be fooled sometimes.

At the same high-class auction where he did so well buying rough country pieces, Don picked up a piece of African sculpture for

$100 and congratulated himself on a good buy. He was teaching at Scotia, a local college, at the time, and took his find in to the people in the art department there. Everyone got excited. What Don had, they said, was an example of a particular sculpturing technique, particular to one specific African tribe. They said that such good examples of it were hard to find and Don was lucky to have made such a great buy.

He packed it into his Volkswagen bus at the end of the day to drive home, but he hadn't settled it in securely, so as he turned a corner, the African sculpture shifted and for the first time he caught sight of the underside of its base and saw that the piece was signed — KOWALSKI.

Kowalski?

Probably some Polish woodcarver whittled it for restaurant decoration, Don says.

Three years later, Don finally sold whittler Kowalski's African sculpture for $35. He'll never buy another piece of sculpture without looking at the bottom, not even at a "good" auction.

In looking over what you intend to bid on, it helps to know certain kinds of flaws are especially likely to turn up in auction pieces. Remember, as we said before, some of the pieces are there because dealers couldn't sell them any other way. If you buy glass or china, check for chips and cracks. Chipped glass is almost worthless, but tiny chips are hard to see except up close. In fact, you can't even count on seeing them. You have to run your finger around the rim of each piece to feel that there are no tiny chips.

Chairs may be the most risky auction buy of all. If the back legs on chairs with curved, steam-bent legs are broken, they can't be fixed. Your response to this may be that no sensible person would buy a bunch of irreparable broken chairs at auction or anyplace else. But it's not a lot of broken chairs that's apt to get you in trouble; it's a set of chairs in good shape except for perhaps one with a broken leg. In a dealer's shop you would probably look closely at the whole set even if you were heaving them down from a pile one at a time, before you made an irrevocable commitment to buy. You would spot a broken leg. But at an auction, even though the chairs are lined up pretty, any buyer who hasn't already learned the hard way tends to think the chairs look like they're in great shape and to assume that the entire set is in good condition. Some dealers and some auctioneers count on it. The attitude is that you can get rid of a broken chair by putting it on auction. Some fool will buy it. In the beginning, Don bought many sets of "broke back" chairs, and he has sold them to auctioneers or run them through a sale to get rid of them. Now he says he makes "a religious habit" of checking every chair before bidding. Don believes that the majority of sets of chairs you see at antiques auctions have broken back legs. When you think about it, he says, it makes sense. You know that rearing back in a chair, shifting all the weight to its back legs, is eventually going to break it. And you know that over the period of seventy-five years or so of a chair's existence, somebody's bound to rear back. The problem is so common that it affects the value of the unbroken chairs, too. A set of six unbroken chairs is a prize. Even a set of four is valuable. Let's say you have a set of four with curved, steam-bent back legs, worth $300 if all the chairs are intact. That averages out to a value of $75 per chair. If one of the four in the set is a broken-back chair, the remaining three chairs are worth not $75 each, but only $15 or $20 each.

Broken chairs aren't the only pieces notorious as "auction merchandise." You are also likely to find chests that have been refinished on the outside but are broken or have no runners inside. In fact, dealers refer to an "auction finish," which means a piece has been dumped into a stripping tank and then covered with a coat of something cheap. The idea is to make it look good on the outside. It's like selling used cars. If you have to put money into a used car before you sell it, you won't spend money to fix the motor, you'll spend it to paint the car because buyers respond to the cosmetic improvement. In an auction, bargain hunting buyers won't pay the extra for quality work that they would in a shop. That's why an auction finish is put only on the outside of the piece; the interior would never be stripped and finished.

Other auction merchandise might include phonographs that don't play. Although the auctioneer tells you this, it is implied that they can be fixed easily, when in reality they need expensive gears. Old radios can trap you, too. They needed a variety of different kinds of tubes. You may bid on an old radio, expecting only to have to find one or two replacement tubes, but when you get it home you discover that all the tubes are missing. Inspecting the merchandise would prevent a knowledgeable buyer from making this mistake. But even the pros sometimes buy without looking closely. And things like broken chairs keep showing up at auctions because people keep buying them. Don says you can make money even on such items at auction because "all it takes is two people bidding who haven't looked."

What makes people who know better buy foolishly at auctions? And, if experts do it, what hope do beginners have? Call it "auction fever" or call it lapsed judgment, but something about the excitement and competition of bidding catches people in its momentum and makes them behave for a time as if the signals they are giving the auctioneer don't have anything to do with money coming out of their pockets. That's why we emphasize doing your rational thinking ahead of time and writing down your top bids, because in the heat of the moment, even the pros can get sucked into giving too much. As Don put it, explaining how he paid too much for the oak secretary that was only a shell, "I put my hand up one more time and the next thing I knew it was up another hundred dollars."

For some people it isn't always simply a matter of beating someone else out of a desirable item; some people hate to lose anything, even a bad deal, to someone else in competition. For them, and you may be one of these, bidding turns into a determination to win the bid, with any sense of the value of what you are bidding on forgotten. If this happens to you more than occasionally, maybe you will need to have someone else handle auction buying for you. Whenever people ask him for advice about auctions, Don says, "If you can't stand to lose, stay away. You're an auctioneer's dream." Not only that, if you go to many auctions, you become the sweet dream of the entire community of auctioneers, because the word gets out on the grapevine that once you start to bid, you're "on for keeps." And *that,* Don says, tempts many auctioneers to keep "finding bids" even when no one else is bidding. To do it, they simply acknowledge another bid, even though no one has really made one. It's hard to tell if you're sitting in a roomful of people and the auctioneer is going fast whether he's really getting bids other than yours or not.

If you lose your sense only now and then, you should get along by setting your mental limits as we suggested and accepting the fact that even when you're a professional, now and then you're going to pull a boner.

When you do, obviously you could simply refuse to pay if you discover the mistake before you load up at the end of the sale, but among the professionals, it's considered a matter of honor to live with your mistake. And if you refuse very often to take a piece on which you won the bid, word will get around among auctioneers — that grapevine again. You could actually be banned from more auctions; they might refuse to give you a number when you show up. The graceful way out of such a mistake among the pros is to pay for the piece and leave it behind, telling the auctioneer to sell it for you at the next sale. Incredibly, sometimes you make money. Sometimes when you ask to leave a piece behind, a sympathetic auctioneer will volunteer to let you off the hook, but don't count on it. If you make a beginning mistake so costly that you think it will keep you from developing your business, you could explain, with many apologies, and decline to pay for the piece. You probably can get away with it once without ruining your reputation, certainly no more. It's far better to restrain your impulses and look before you buy — no matter what. Start out professionally.

As a professional, you should sit right up front, where the auctioneer can see when you bid. In that location you won't be distracted by the wandering and conversations of people who are there mostly for entertainment. The myth that important dealers sit in the back and bid in subtle signals not detectable by the rest of the crowd, so no one will realize that what's on the block is valuable enough for important dealers to want it is nonsense. Anytime you get a number of dealers and knowledgeable collectors in an auction crowd, they are going to know when a recognizably valuable piece shows up. The misconception probably comes from the fact that sometimes if a well-known dealer is at a sale only for a few big money items, he sits

in the back or uses subtle bidding signals so that amateurs won't bid up the piece on the theory that if a well-known dealer wants it, it must be a good buy.

It's worth mentioning here that as a beginner, you should not try to make your buying decisions at auction by watching what a dealer bids for and then raising. Most dealers have seen a new competitor slide into a seat behind them and "follow the leader" on bidding. When this happens, the established dealer gets done out of his load. Naturally, if he catches on to what's happening, he'll try to hang the copycat with a load of trash.

When Don caught a newcomer to the business raising him on everything he bid for, he immediately began bidding on all kinds of things he didn't want. The woman raised him — and won the bid — every time. When the sale was over, after looking at some of the culls she had bought, she said to Don, "You were bidding on these. Wouldn't you like to buy them for your last bid?"

Don said, "No, I don't need them."

"Then why were you bidding," she asked.

"Just doin' the auctioneer a favor," he said.

She learned the hard way not to bid using someone else's knowledge. It's simply not acceptable in the business to copy one specific dealer hoping to be instructed by what he is doing. Ironically, the same dealer who will hang you if he finds you raising his bids will probably sit next to you and give you advice on everything that comes up if you ask for help. Don spends a lot of time at auctions (sitting up front, of course) helping people new to the business avoid bad buys.

He has learned that another advantage to sitting in front is being able to see the merchandise better. This is especially important if you are bidding on boxes full of articles. You need to be sure that nobody has gone through the contents and taken out the piece you wanted most in the box sometime between when you looked through it and when it went up for bidding.

Also, being up front gives you a chance to watch and understand the auctioneer and let him get to know you. You'll do better at an auction if the auctioneer likes you.

And no matter how closely he sees your face, the auctioneer won't like you very much if you go against the basic auction rules of bidding, paying, and hauling.

How Auctions Work

Auctioneers are no different from anyone else. When they have a job to do, they want it to go smoothly and they appreciate bidders who help keep business moving along. When you want to bid, do it quickly and clearly. Sara remembers being terribly embarrassed just for being in the audience at an auction where a lot of novices were sticking in bids just as the auctioneer was knocking down each sale. He stopped and lectured the entire group in a tone clearly not intended to entertain. "If you want to bid," he said, "speak up and do it when it's time. We can't fool around up here while you decide what you want to do." Don't try to change your mind either: you can't *unbid,* though, of course, any bid can be your last bid.

When you signed in, you were probably given a card with a number on it. Each time you win a bid, show the card and call out the number so that the auction bookkeeper can write down what you bought and for what price. At the end of the sale, all your purchases will be totalled and you will pay for everything at once. When you buy small objects, they are often passed to you by one of the auctioneer's helpers as you win the bids, but you won't be able to get to large objects until the sale is over.

Find out ahead of time what the terms of payment will be. Terms vary with the auction and with who is buying. Auctioneers usually refuse out-of-state checks. Some will also refuse in-state checks from strangers. The one way many auctioneers will take checks from people they don't know is when the check is accompanied by a letter from the bank on which it is drawn stating how large a check will be honored. Auctioneers will always accept cash and travelers cheques joyfully. If you are traveling to an auction where you don't know what the usual terms of payment are, call ahead and ask.

Ask also about how soon after sale the merchandise must be removed. Often it must be removed immediately. This means you must either go prepared to haul what you buy or forgo buying anything that won't fit into your Volkswagen Beetle.

These seem like little things, but your failure to know and follow the norm at an auction will earn you a reputation almost immediately as a troublemaker. Auctioneers who recognize you will make your being at the sale unpleasant, if they let you in at all. It's important to understand that at an auction the auctioneer is an absolute monarch. He can bestow favors at will. As we continue this discussion of how auctions work, we'll point out a number of ways the auctioneer can help or hurt you.

For instance, in a bidding situation, you'd think that whatever merchandise was offered would go at whatever price the crowd would pay, high or low. It certainly will go as high as people will pay, but if bids are coming in very low for the value of the merchandise, buyers do not automatically get the bargains. Auctioneers have ways to avoid selling at overly low prices and they have ways to run prices up. It's an important skill because an auctioneer who can't get enough money for what he sells won't have many people hiring his services.

After you have attended a few sales, you will notice that all the items aren't always sold. In some cases the auctioneer may decide that a piece isn't bringing bids at the level it should, and he'll simply put it aside. Other times, bidding will begin so sluggishly that the auctioneer gets disgusted and puts the item aside. Don likes to make a quick *low* bid on everything he wants. The auctioneer appreciates quick first bids to get things moving. And even though Don's bid is low, the auctioneer will sometimes close the sale quickly to Don, before somebody else gets caught up in competing for the piece, bidding up its price. Don is especially prone to do this when he's at a sale to buy a lot of merchandise. Of course, auctioneers he deals with regularly know this and will give up a little in price on some pieces in favor of moving volume more rapidly. Still, there is a limit to how low the prices will go.

At a sale when bids were coming in too low, Don has seen an auctioneer say, "Obviously you people are not serious about buying here," and stop the sale.

Theoretically, when an auction is advertised as an "absolute auction," it means that everything must be sold, no matter how low the bidding, but it doesn't always work that way.

At fine city auctions, for instance, most of the goods have reserve bids placed on them in writing by the owners of the merchandise. If bidding from the floor does not at least match the reserve bid, the piece will not be sold during the auction, but will be returned to the owner or offered for sale again later. At regular auctions, haulers who bring in goods don't want to have to pack them up unsold and haul them off again, but often they have to get a certain minimum price on better items. If they are working on consignment, they have to make the consignment price plus the fee of the auction house before they can even think about profit. If bidding is too low, they may "bid" on their own pieces. This keeps those pieces from going for the low bids, and the haulers load up again after the sale to try again at another auction somewhere else. In effect, the goods were offered, didn't make the asking price (which bidders don't know about) and were returned to the hauler. No money changed hands. Obviously, the auctioneer knows and goes along with it. In such cases, the haulers may reload their stuff and go to five or six different auctions to get rid of everything before heading home.

When someone buys a load of antiques from Don to haul to an auction, Don will give a "buy-back" price on some items. If he has sold the hauler a table for $100, for instance, he may tell the hauler that if things don't go well at the auction, he's willing to buy back the table for $75. In a sense, Don's offer to buy back at $75 is an opening bid because the hauler (with the auctioneer's cooperation) isn't going to let the table go unless he gets more than $75. Any less and he might as well just haul it back and resell it to Don. In principle it is exactly the same as the written reserve bids at fine auctions.

As we've said, auctioneers have been known to stop sales when bids were unacceptably low on the day's offerings. But they're more likely to "grab bids off the wall," play acting, so to speak, as though people were bidding vigorously for an item, when in fact no one is. Don has seen auctioneers run a piece from $100 to $4,000 or $5,000 — and sell it — without having any real bids until the end. Other times, Don has known that he and the auctioneer were the only bidders on a piece, but he's gone along with the "bidding" as long as it stayed within the limits he'd set for himself because he knew the auctioneer needed to sell the piece and also needed to get a certain minimum amount for it. Don would say that's not just Christian charity. He reasons that if he helps the auctioneers, they will help him. They do.

Sometimes auctioneers will knock down a quick sale to him at a low price when they might have tried instead for more and higher bids. And sometimes they will refrain from cajoling the audience to go higher if Don has made what is known as a "knock-out bid." When Don makes a knock-out bid, he skips his usual and expected low opening bid and immediately bids high. This discourages other bidders from getting in, and, in the long run, the piece actually goes cheaper than if it had started for less. The advantage to the auctioneer is that it goes quickly. Here is an example. The piece was a primitive blanket chest with drawers, mounted on a low frame, known as a mule chest. It was a northern piece, at a southern auction. Interest was not high because of that, but Don knew that at "the Yankee price" it was worth $400. He opened bidding at $200, a high opening for him, and got it at that price. Later, he sold it off the truck to a dealer for $400. The dealer sold it to an appreciative Yankee at a profit.

If he had let the bidding drop down to $100 before getting in, other buyers might have begun bidding and run the price above $400. Although that would have probably suited the auctioneer, he was glad to let it go to Don at a fair price at least partly because Don is a buyer whom he knows, trusts, likes, and with whom he regularly does business. Don tries a knock-out bid when he wants something he doesn't think he has much chance of getting because it probably will go too high. His knock-out bid is basically his maximum price. It's kind of a one-shot gamble. If someone raises, he won't bid again.

Knowing all this, you may wonder why merchandise sometimes moves briskly, without obstruction from the auctioneer, at noticeably low prices. It doesn't always happen this way, but the reason could be that the auctioneer has opened the bid himself and is, himself, trying to buy pieces cheap. Later, he'll sell them somewhere else, probably at another sale where he is the auctioneer. His commission would be smaller, but he would make up for it by earning a profit when he resold the pieces. In buying this way, the auctioneer knocks down the item on a house number. This means that the auctioneer simply pretends to be getting bids or has a confederate in the group actually bidding. When the bid is "won" and he pounds the gavel and tells the record keeper the number to which the item should be marked sold, the auctioneer uses a number he has assigned to himself or the house. Of course, the people in the audience don't know it's a house number. If the auctioneer already owns the piece, he can use the same trick to try to hold back advertised pieces that he doesn't want to sell this way. It's a device to deal with the fact that legally any piece that is advertised for auction must be offered at the sale. One way an auctioneer selling something of his own can apparently meet the legal obligation is to offer it and then use the house number to prevent a real sale if he thinks bids are not high enough.

Laws about auction buying and selling vary. If you are going into business, or for that matter collecting seriously, learn how the laws work in the states in which you expect to buy and sell. In many states if you suspect you are losing buys to the auctioneer himself or are being run up by a nonexistent bidder, you can ask for the identity of the other bidder. Whether the auctioneer is trying to protect a price for a client, to boost the price on something of his own, or to buy an advertised piece from the auction goods for himself cheaply is beside the point for you. What matters is that when you can't buy some advertised merchandise you expected to be able to get at good prices, the auctioneer's involvement may be a factor.

Having told you that, we hasten to add that nobody who wants to stay in the business actually challenges an auctioneer when that seems to be happening. A collector or occasional buyer is more likely to do it. To work effectively in the antiques business you have little choice but to go along with the customs in the area where you are operating. And it is accepted custom that at most auctions, the prices on big-money pieces will be protected for a variety of reasons and in a number of ways. This means you probably can't steal a sixteen-pane walnut corner cupboard, a period secretary, rare signed pottery, or listed artist oil paintings, though you might get them for decent prices. But even at auctions where such items are not going to be allowed to drop below an established minimum, *you will find other bargains, especially among the pieces no one is paying much attention to.*

In looking for bargains, another practice of some auctioneers that you should understand is what we have mentioned earlier as "packing sales." Sometimes auctioneers will accept a reduced commission on estate sales in return for being permitted to bring in some of their own merchandise. We said earlier that people tend to pay more at estate sales. There's something about merchandise scattered throughout a house and around the grounds of a property that makes it more appealing to some buyers. The auctioneer finds his own merchandise sells better and at a higher price in the estate-sale situation than it would otherwise. The problem here is misrepresentation. As a buyer you are led to assume that everything for sale belonged to the estate. Yet the auctioneer does not actually lie. Your assumptions do the job.

An advertisement for "an estate auction at the J. Johnson homeplace" doesn't actually say that the goods have anything to do with J. Johnson. It merely tells you where the auction will be held. You can't count on the word "estate" meaning anything except that some of what is sold was once part of somebody's estate. For whatever reason, "estate" gives people a positive feeling toward a sale that has nothing to do with anything. We can't underestimate the power of a beautiful spring day and birds singing in the trees, either.

In packing a sale, the auctioneer usually supplies his own merchandise to fill the gaps in the house and on the grounds. For instance, one auctioneer makes sure there is a riding mower at all the sales he works. Often they go for anywhere from $100 to $250. Clearly they're not antiques; it is likely they won't run well. But they sell so well that the auctioneer in question says "it would be a sin not to have one at every sale."

You'll always find old guns and coins, generally brought in by the auctioneer, too. If the living room or a bedroom doesn't have much to sell in it, the auctioneer will bring in beds, chairs, and other appropriate merchandise, knowing that the notion of an "estate" sale will incline people to pay more than they otherwise would for the pieces.

Even in legitimate estate sales, with executors, that aren't heavily packed, switching occurs. One example of how it works is the estate sale of a woman whose Victorian living room suite was famous in the area. When the woman died, her executor took it and replaced it with a plain, much less valuable Victorian living room suite of her own. The replacement suite brought an enormous amount of money based on hearsay reputation. Obviously, it had to have been bought by someone with no clear sense of value in Victorian furniture.

It's hard to overstate the crazy prices merchandise sometimes brings at estate sales. One auctioneer explains it by saying, "When it's rolling, it's rolling." A sale he held recently, on a pretty homeplace with birds and sunshine in spring got to rolling so well that boxes of junk that ordinarily would have gone for a couple of bucks all moved at a minimum of $10 each. And somehow a box of trash intended for the dump got held up and somebody bought that, too.

At that same sale somebody paid in the neighborhood of $100 for an old Snapper lawnmower that had been run to death. It was in such bad shape that its internal parts were in a bucket beside the casing. It was worth, at most, $20 for the parts.

Another time, during a sale less than two miles from Don's shop, an oak wall-phone went for $400. Don had a dozen wall-phones in his shop, many of them identical to the one at the sale, for $200.

When it's rolling, it's rolling.

One auctioneer who understands this actually took a few sales for free in exchange for the use of a beautiful old empty country house that he could fill up with his merchandise to hold fake house sales.

You may find these little tricks of questionable morality, but as a buyer you need to know about them. They are part of the whole antiques business system, just as pickers and shop owners and collectors are.

Auctioneers are no more larcenous than their customers. They want to sell nothing for something. Customers want to buy something for nothing. The same customers who are gleeful over making a steal at auction become indignant about auctioneers running up bids. Auctioneers really aren't bad guys. They are gamblers by nature, which is probably how they got into what they do. They live from deal to deal, sometimes clearing huge amounts of money and sometimes losing nearly as much. Most of them would like to buy big loads and sell for whatever each piece brings naturally, but if they have lost money on the previous two or three auctions, they cannot afford to lose on the next one — and that's where the tricks come in.

For the professionals it's a game, a battle of wits. You, as a customer, are trying to get merchandise for as little as possible; the auctioneer is trying for a good price, sometimes on questionable merchandise. Ideally, the two sides meet somewhere near the middle.

As long as you are looking and buying in a businesslike way and understand what may be going on well enough not to be seduced by the fun of going to sales, none of these things really hurts you. In fact, at *any* sale, when everyone else is paying attention to something different, you may find a bargain among the things people aren't buying.

Some people are so distrustful of sales in auction houses being rigged that they buy only at estate sales; others are so negative about "estate" sales that they will buy only at auction houses. If you want to make money, you can't get so exclusive. When you know what you are doing, you can find bargains — and gyps — anywhere.

Buying at auction is the most complex kind of buying for antiques. What we have to say next about yard sales, flea markets, and so on should seem comparatively simple.

CHAPTER 5

How to Buy Antiques

The Cline rule of success in the antiques business is simple. *Develop a sense of what everything in the world is worth. When you see it for less, buy.*

Cline's corollary is simple, too. *The average person does not know the value of what he or she has to sell.*

Buying is what the antique business is all about. If you don't love shopping, this is the wrong business for you, because active buying is the only way you can have something to sell. The antiques business differs from other businesses in this. If you have a country store, for instance, you can decide to carry certain items and then simply reorder them as inventory gets low. With antiques, the inventory changes with every sale and purchase you make. You can't just order up a dozen oak chairs or six pine tables. You have to find the merchandise before you can buy it. Fortunately, most people who get into the business do so because they love that finding-buying process.

With antiques, it's hard to separate buying and selling because often they happen within minutes of each other. A customer who is around when a new piece comes in may want to buy it before you've even gotten it off the truck. Sara's desk is a good case in point. She went to Cline's looking for a big oak desk. Just as she got out of the car, Don was paying a picker for a load of furniture which included a desk that was exactly what Sara had in mind. Sara paid Don and gave the picker a few dollars to haul the desk to her house. It was never even off the truck during the five minutes or so that Don owned it. Things like that happen all the time at Cline's.

Given the unusually close relationship between buying and selling, we recognize that it is somewhat unnatural and artificial to write about them separately, in two different chapters. We're going to do it anyway so that we can keep sharply focused on some important points that must be made about each.

Before we go into detail about buying in specific situations such as yard sales and auctions, let's look at buying in general. We are concerned with two problems: learning to sense the market and developing your own buying style.

People in antiques work from either of two basically different philosophies of buying. One is to buy only when you can make a killing; the other is to buy whatever you know you can sell. Although both are versions of the basic buy-low, sell-high dictum, they are quite different ways of operating. The first approach usually assumes lower turnover with a greater profit on each transaction; the second implies less profit on some sales but more of them. Here is an example of the first approach.

Don often does business with a dealer who passes up chances to buy even desirable merchandise if it isn't a deal that's too good to be believed. He made such a deal just about the time old jukeboxes were becoming hot on the market. He found a warehouse *full* of discarded jukeboxes and bought them all at $15 each. Part of his deal included continuing to store them in the warehouse, so he didn't even have to haul them away. He began selling those jukeboxes for hundreds of dollars apiece. To give you an idea of what a fantastically good deal he made, some of the jukeboxes were visible in the windows of the warehouse in which they were stored. As the public interest in jukeboxes grew, motorists who saw them began stopping and trying to buy them from the previous owner whose house was on the same property. The offers were for so much money that the dealer ended up hauling away his remaining jukeboxes to keep the previous owner from getting any more upset than she already was.

Every dealer dreams of such buys but not too many limit their purchasing to those rare opportunities.

The other approach, buying anything you think you can sell, which happens to be Don's style, insures much more activity. Don likes it that way. And his buying style results in some bonuses, too. His experience with woodstoves is a good example. During the years when people were converting to oil heat, Don had a chance to buy a woodstove practically every time he picked up a load anywhere. Typically, old Quarter Cline got them for anywhere from twenty-five cents to a dollar. They would have brought more than that as scrap, but nobody was showing up offering to haul them away at scrap prices, so the market was wide open to Don, even at his below-scrap offers. He bought so many that he filled one shed with woodstoves. And — you can see what's coming, can't you? — then the energy crisis caught us by surprise. Don started selling those stoves for $50 to $100 each. There's more to this story, though. When Americans began to take the energy crisis seriously, manufacturers started developing high-tech woodstoves that burned longer on less wood and required infrequent feeding. They were clearly superior to old-style woodstoves. The market for Don's old stoves disappeared. Today, he sometimes gives them away. That's not bad because he's already made a respectable profit on those he sold when demand was high.

As we said, both philosophies are based on one of the oldest stock market adages, "Buy low, sell high." No matter how you get to it, the only way to make money is to sell your merchandise for more than you paid for it.

Estimating the Market

This brings us to considerations of market. In settling on your own buying style, you have to develop a knack for estimating the market. You have to learn to think not only about where it has been and where it is now, but also about where it probably will go next. And since you're not going to be able to guess right every time, you're going to need to learn how to hedge your bets in buying. Here are some instances of what we mean.

When Don was first getting into antiques, one of his personal interests was old bottles and fruit jars. At the peak of public interest in them, he paid as much as $10 each for jars. But then the market for bottles and jars died. People wouldn't pay even $1 for a bottle. If his buying had been confined to bottles and jars, he would have been in trouble when the market changed. But the baskets and boxes that once held the bottles became popular. Since he'd gotten them by buying the bottles, Don had boxes and baskets to sell when customers lost interest in bottles. Also, he had been acquiring logical "go-withs," small items other than boxes, baskets, and bottles that fit into the popular country-store look, such as old signs and advertising. They've been hot ever since, with values steadily increasing.

In 1973, for instance, Don bought a Piedmont Cigarette sign for fifty cents at a farm sale, where he found it nailed up over a hog pen. He cleaned it and hung it in his bedroom until he was married and his wife suggested he take it down. Later, he sold it for $40. Today he could sell it for $100. At that same sale, he paid $10 for an 1858 dated fruit jar. Two years later, he couldn't move it for $2. But bottles and jars are beginning to come back into vogue. He could sell that jar for $4 right now. Buying a variety of goods is how Don keeps up with the changing market.

Another example of how tastes in antiques change in the marketplace is the current popularity of painted, decorated furniture. A few years ago, a painted, decorated blanket chest would sell simply as an old chest. Whoever bought it probably cussed the paint, stripped the chest, and refinished it. Today, such pieces are considered folk art — worth tens of times more with the paint and decorations on. A Tennessee collector bought two blanket chests elaborately decorated for $400. A decorator magazine showed the chests in an article about the collector's home. The collector got a call from someone in California who had seen the article. "I'm calling to buy those chests," the Californian said.

"I'm sorry, they're not for sale."

The California man persisted. "You don't understand, I mean to have those chests, at any price."

And the collector persisted, too. "They're not for sale at any price."

A few days later, the Californian showed up in Tennessee. "I came for the chests," he said.

"I told you, they're not for sale."

The California man asked if he could see the chests anyway and the owner supposed it would be okay, since the traveler had come so far. It seemed churlish to refuse. But they were definitely not for sale. After looking them over, the Californian wrote out a check for $30,000, which, it turned out, was enough to buy two old elaborately decorated blanket chests that were definitely not for sale.

And, surely, across the South people with nicely refinished blanket chests are crying, vowing never again to scrape the paint and decorations off another piece, no matter what their personal taste about such things.

One of Don's mistakes about the market happened because he let his personal taste affect his judgment. He likes old porcelain signs, but he doesn't like *English* porcelains. In going through a load of merchandise that was mostly English, he came across a tobacco sign with a pretty girl on it, which he bought for $40. Minutes later, he sold it for $60 to a customer who'd seen it being unloaded. Before the week was done, he learned that the sign wasn't English at all. It was a very rare early pretobacco trust porcelain with a value of about $300. His distaste for the English signs had led him to dismiss it on the assumption it was just more of the same.

A Matter of Many Tastes

Letting your personal taste have too much influence on your business decisions is a real danger in antiques. As we worked on this book, Don said repeatedly that we had to stress flexibility because tastes in the marketplace change. Most people who go into the antiques business begin with what they know and like, just as Don began with what appealed to him. As your business expands, your interests and likes will probably expand with it. But, like Don, you will have to develop a calculating sense on the market. Sometimes it doesn't matter what you like; what matters is what your customers like. Unfortunately, the likes of some customers will change with the fancies and fads of the times. Today they can't get enough country. Tomorrow it may be Victorian. If you see the market for the things you like going soft, you'll either have to make room for the next wave of taste or give up the business.

If you're still struggling with today, how do you know what's going to be valuable tomorrow? Some people seem to have better intuitions than others, but much of what they know is rooted in reading and listening. Some of it is simply being willing to buy a bargain, risk a mistake, and then waiting to see what happens. Some of it is pure luck.

Here's a classic case of a combination of being willing to buy a bargain and getting lucky. About five years ago, in the contents of an old shed, a friend of Don's came across a boxful of strange woodcarvings. They were walking sticks with grotesque heads of Negroes be-

ing strangled carved into the handles. Folk art had not yet become a big item, but Don's friend kept the carvings, even though Don would have paid $100 for them. Recently, the friend turned down an offer of $5,000 for them. Since then, at a yard sale, he found a boxful of more such carvings, even better, along with all the tools, which he bought for $5 from a woman who considered them junk. Buying junk and selling rare folk art offer the largest profits in the business today, if you can recognize the potential before others do.

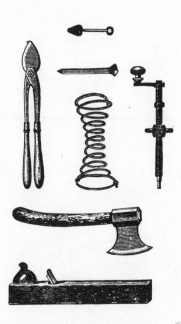

If you follow developments in cultural taste (which is what influences our buying habits), you'll find that fads don't just spring up, even though it seems as though they do. A lot of intellectuals aren't going to like this, but fads really start at the academic level. When we began publicly emphasizing the value of our individual cultural heritages, it was just a matter of time until whatever artifacts remained from those heritages would be viewed as valuable. Similarly, anyone watching the "back to the land" movement that began in the late sixties and early seventies, with its emphasis on simpler living and returning to earlier way of doing things could have guessed it would contribute to a market for antique tools, pottery, cookware, and furniture.

More clues come from magazines that shape our tastes. *Country Living* and other decorator magazines have sent countless people to antique shops looking for old iron skillets, quilts, rag rugs, rope beds, painted furniture, and whatever else they've featured. Magazines such as *Yankee* and *Southern Living* that emphasize regional history and its artifacts influence taste, too.

As a buyer, you hope to have caught on to trends in taste *before* they get to be full-color spreads in national magazines. Local newspapers, regional publications, and the interests of all the buyers and sellers you come in contact with are good clues. And don't forget about reading all the antiques trade journals and auctions reports you can find.

Items that are rare or in limited supply will probably increase in value. Anything handmade is a pretty safe bet. As we've said before, you can count on old items native to your area to grow in value *in that area*. This seems to be true even as other values fluctuate with fads. But if local antiques are enjoying a great surge of popularity in your area, be careful about buying them. You will be jumping in at the height of a local fad, paying too much, and you will probably find yourself unable to recoup your investment when the craze slows again.

Within highly specialized areas, you can predict value simply by knowing the field. License plate collectors, for instance, know that 1918 North Carolina license plates are not expensive because large quantities of unsold plates have turned up. Don sells them for $15 each and has many. North Carolina plates from the year 1917 are a different story. They were manufactured out of state; the leftovers were returned to the manufacturer, who probably melted them down to make something else; and their quality was so inferior that most of those still around rusted. Don had to pay $300 to get one for his personal collection. Yet, except for the date, plates for the two years are identical. In this case, knowing the history of the item plus understanding supply and demand will tell you which plates are valuable and which are nearly worthless. Because Don likes license plates, he buys more of them than his business sense says he should. Advertising signs with nationwide interest are worth buying in large lots; the market for North Carolina license plates is more limited. Rarity plus demand clearly increases value. Age may or may not.

Just because a piece is old doesn't mean it's valuable. Empire furniture, that heavy, ungraceful, clunky furniture, is a good example. Ten years ago, an 1840 Empire chest with chips in the veneer was worth about $30. Today it's still only worth about $30. It was ugly when it was new; now it is old and ugly.

On the other hand, a 1940 beer can that wouldn't have cost more than a quarter with the beer in it at the time might be worth $100 today, not because it's beautiful or even old enough to be a true antique, but because collectors want it. By these lights, presumably you could increase the value of your 1840 Empire chest by eliminating all the others. Maybe it wouldn't seem so ugly if it were the only one left. And you could get it featured in a decorator magazine as the newest "old look" so that many people would want it.

With antiques, as with beachfront property, when there isn't any more, the value of what's already available goes up — provided people still want to go to the beach.

The Time Factor

Time is your friend in this business. If you make mistakes, time will bail you out. Good antiques are always valuable, even when their popularity is not growing at an astronomical rate. If the antique is good quality, somebody will always want it. A good example of this is the contrast in current value between country antiques and something like walnut Victorian furniture. In the past ten years, the country pieces have shown the greatest jump in what they bring — from a couple of dollars to more than $200 for pine tables, for example. The Victorian pieces cost more ten years ago and their value hasn't increased as much since then, but they are still in demand at modestly increased prices. You'll always be able to sell a good Victorian piece at a good price. In fact, with so many people restoring Victorian houses and some decorator magazines featuring them, Victorian furniture and art prices are rising again. Some dealers believe that country has peaked and Victorian is coming on. Don doesn't really want to believe it because he has done well with country furniture and it's more in line with his personal tastes, but you'll find more Victorian pieces in his shop these days than you once would have.

You can see in all this a reflection of the fact that two kinds of customers buy antiques: a hard core of regulars who know what they want and buy it regardless of what is going on in popular taste, and people who follow fads and trends. If you buy to cater to both classes of customer, you broaden your market and provide yourself with a more stable base than if you only respond to fads or buy only sure things.

One area of faddism that Don considers especially risky is artificially created collectibles: collector plates, Avon bottles, specially minted coins, limited editions of porcelain knick-knacks, and specially advertised lots of signed sculpture are examples of this. They are marketed to collectors with the implication that as time passes they will become increasingly valuable, just as antiques do, because they were produced in limited quantities. But it will be a long time (50 or even a hundred years) before they are old enough to be interesting, and even then they may not appeal to anybody else. We aren't suggesting that you ought not to buy these things if you happen to like them, but don't do it expecting them to become valuable anytime soon. Some will go up. Most will probably go down. It may be worthwhile to buy a box full of knick-knacks for a few dollars, but don't pay a lot for them and expect to make any money.

Developing Your Instincts

If all this leaves you wondering how one knows what is a good buy and what isn't, you're not alone. Dealers make mistakes every day. We could fill an entire book with stories of bad buys and another book with stories of good buys that got away. But the people who make these mistakes are right more often than they are wrong. In addition to watching the culture, reading, and talking to dealers and collectors, you have one more thing to help you buy well — your own sense of taste and quality. As you work with antiques, handling good pieces and bad, and become knowledgeable about them, you will find that you develop a reliable sense of what to buy and what to leave alone, just as people who eat in many fine restaurants learn to discern good cooking from bad, and people who hear many kinds of music learn to distinguish the good from the mediocre in any category of music. The more you look at good antiques, the more internalized your sense of quality will become. This is why it's good to tour museums and go to as many sales and shows as you can, even when you have no intention of buying anything.

At least some of Don's instincts come from an early exposure to antiques, even though he was indifferent at the time. People in his family liked fine antiques. He remembers, for instance, driving south from Vermont one time with his Aunt Clara in the back of the car madly scraping paint off a chair so that they could drop it off to be caned at a school for the blind in Raleigh when they arrived home. Although his own taste developed toward rough country pieces rather than "fine" antiques, and even though he more or less backed into the business almost by accident, the experience of his younger days has provided him with the ability to separate quality from junk.

Having talked about some general principles of buying, let's turn now to the specific situations and people on whom you will be practicing those principles: suppliers, pickers, and yard sales.

Finding Yard Sale Goodies

As a beginner with limited capital, yard sales can be a good source of bargains for antiques and collectibles, especially if you become highly knowledgeable in some specialized areas so that you recognize the deals when you find them. But shopping at yard sales takes a lot of time. After you've become established and your business grows, you won't have as much time to spend that way and at that point you may switch to having pickers do it for you. (Conversely, if you find that you enjoy yard sales so much you don't want to give them up to run a business, you can act as a picker, shopping the sales for people who prefer to stay with their businesses. It's a nice way to buy for dealers if you don't have the nerve to door-knock, and you can do it without feeling guilty.) Whether yard sales are worth pursuing at all depends on where you live. Yard sales are not equally good in all areas. The value of pursuing them may depend on what people offer at yard sales in your part of the country.

We gave you a hint about buying at yard sales when we talked about how to have one. We told you to expect some people to show up early — even before the announced opening time of the sale. These are usually serious buyers. If you are going to do well shopping at yard sales, you will have to become one of them and get there as early as they do, before the good things are bought and carried away. Don's first rule is *go early*.

His second rule is *keep going*. Every yard sale you attend isn't going to reward you with wonderful bargains; some aren't going to reward you at all. Don knows a collector of Boy Scout memorabilia who hits as many yard sales as he can. During one depressing period, he went to sale after sale after sale without finding anything. Less persistent people might have given up. Fortunately, this collector persisted and at three sales in the same day he found absolutely super collections of Boy Scout memorabilia at low, yard sale prices.

Don's third rule is *haggle*. But he's a little soft on this one. He thinks it's bad manners to beat down a seller if the goods are already underpriced; in those cases he'd rather just pay. However, often prices are not all that low. People usually don't expect to get the prices they put on yard sale items, because they know that for many yard sale addicts, dickering over price is part of the entertainment. Even if you are more comfortable just paying what a seller first asks, learn to make a lower offer. You will be amazed at how much of the time you get the item for less. There are several reasons for this.

First, as Don has often noted, most people do not know the market value of what they have to sell. Even if they do, they sometimes are more interested in just getting rid of things than in making money. Anything they don't sell at a yard sale has to be lugged back inside, and the space where it used to be probably is already filled up with something else. Finally, even knowledgeable people who are selling antiques at yard sales to make money sometimes come down on price because they can afford to. They have almost no overhead. So offer a lower price. Often it will pay off, and even when it doesn't, the worst that can happen is the seller will refuse it and you'll have to pay the full asking price.

In spring and summer, yard sales break out like chicken pox in first grade. You can't possibly get to them all and after a few times browsing through plastic diaper buckets, broken strollers, and old hair dryers, you won't even want to get to them all. How do you figure out which ones are worth hunting up? Newspaper classified advertisements help sometimes, though you can't take every ad that says "antiques" seriously because some people will use that word to draw a crowd even when the oldest thing in the yard was made out of chrome and formica sometime during 1970. We have seen ads for "antique" television sets, "antique" ten-speed bicycles, and even "antique" plastic dishes. Used this way, all the word "antique" means for sure if that the item is scrungy or broken or doesn't work and the owner doesn't want it anymore. If the ad is more specific and offers something like "antique Victorian dining chairs," you may be on to something worthwhile or you may not be on to anything but a bunch of broken chairs, but it will be a lead worth checking. After you've shopped yard sales for a while, you'll find that sales are being advertised regularly at some addresses and after going to a couple, you'll know whether they're consistently good or consistently just collections of odds and ends gathered up by someone who wants pin money. (If a telephone number is given, call a day before the sale. Some sellers will let you have something you especially want early.)

The general address of a sale can be another clue. You can expect legitimate bargains in the older parts of town, where people may be selling old furniture out of their houses to make way for something new. If you are looking for collectibles, you may also do well in the more affluent parts of town. Where you're apt to be disappointed is in the suburbs and areas where young families with children are mostly selling each other their outgrown baby goods, unused basketball hoops, and extra wedding gifts such as crock pots.

Buying Out of Homes

A moving sale is worth checking out in almost any part of town, especially if antiques are mentioned in the ad, because there is a general desire to get rid of things as quickly as possible. These factors will figure into the prices. Sara has owned, sold, and rebought some pieces of oak furniture and iron cookware three times because

of long-distance moves. She has sold for a few hundred dollars family heirlooms worth several times that, because the cost of hauling them from one coast to another was prohibitive and because she was too busy and tired and disgusted to wait for a buyer who would pay more. Moving makes people a little crazy. Sometimes it seems more important to give an old piece to someone who will care for it than to look around for the highest bidder. On the other hand, lots of people have an exaggerated view of what their furniture is worth, especially if it has sentimental family value. You won't be able to buy their things for a bargain unless, possibly, you go back a day or so after the sale and they're still stuck with a lot of furniture that they can't afford to move. Go to moving sales if you hear about them. And be very sweet and sympathetic. No telling what you'll pick up.

When people move, and at other times too, some of them elect to sell items from their homes without having a sale, especially if they know some of their antiques and collectibles might be valuable. They ask a dealer to come to their house to see the merchandise. As you become known as an antiques dealer, you can expect such calls, too. It can be a good buying situation, but you need to have developed your sense of what things are worth before you get into it. You also will need a well-developed sense of diplomacy sometimes.

Negotiating Prices

Not all dealers do it this way, but Don's method of handling these in-the-home deals is to try to get the *owner* to put a price on the merchandise. Then Don will either pay or make a counter offer. He has several reasons for doing it this way. Obviously, sometimes he is able to pick up pieces for less money when the owner asks less than he would have been willing to pay. Equally important, he has not wasted time giving a free estimate. Owners of antiques can get tricky. Not wanting to pay an estimator for the knowledge that has come from years of work, they'll call a dealer for offers, then call a competitor and offer their merchandise at the first dealer's price plus 10 percent. All too often, the competitor gets the deal. If Don can't get the owner to name a price, he will usually make an offer before he leaves, but he will state emphatically that it is not a permanent offer, meaning that if the owner shops around trying to sell to other dealers, trying to get more money based on Don's estimate-offer, Don's offer will drop if the owner comes back to him as a last resort.

The need for diplomacy comes up when an owner puts an unrealistically high price on what he wants to sell — asking $1,000 for an Empire sideboard, for instance. Such inflated ideas about what a piece is worth often come from the owner's sentimental attachment to it. Don't run down the merchandise or bluntly say that it isn't worth what the owner is asking. Not only do you hurt feelings unnecessarily, you lose any chance of getting the piece for a more reasonable price. Don has learned that you should make a counter offer even when you are dealing with an asking price that is sentimentally high. Don cites the experience of Tony, a gun trader, who once admired an old shotgun and asked the owner about its price. The man said, "It's been in the family a long time. It's worth about $1,000." Tony said that was a little over his head and let it go. Another gun enthusiast standing next to Tony at the time said to the owner, "Would you take $200 cash for it right now?" The owner did. You can bet Tony will never again fail to make a counter offer on something he wants that's been priced too high.

One reason you want to have the owner set the price is because some people will automatically listen to your offer and then ask for more — sometimes a lot more. They want your offer as a base to begin negotiating. You can't do much about this beyond holding on to your sense of what you are willing to pay and of what you can resell an item for. Here, as in all buying, you need to know not just the general market but also your own customers. You buy for your customers. If you have collectors among your customers, you will find that for them price is not always the most important thing. Don Sutherland, who probably has the best typewriter collection in America, tells a story about finding a typewriter in mint condition and getting sweaty palms because he just knew the owner was going to ask several hundred dollars for it and Sutherland was going to have to pay because that particular typewriter filled a gap in his collection. As it turned out, Sutherland got the typewriter for $5 because it typed on the underside of the platen (it was built before the advent of visible type) and the poor seller thought there was something wrong with it.

The story certainly illustrates Don Cline's assertion that the average person does not know the value of what he has to sell, but it illustrates something equally important to you as a buyer. Money hardly matters to a collector if you've found something that fills out the collection. What this means if you're in someone's home to buy antiques and collectibles is that sometimes you can afford to go along with an asking price higher than you would ordinarily pay, *provided you have a customer you know will pay a correspondingly higher price*. Don recalls once paying $50 for a broad axe, which is more than he would pay ordinarily, because he knew a customer wanted one for a gift and she had said to him, "Get me one even if it costs $75."

Getting back to setting prices, one other way dealers and sellers dance around when neither wants to make the first move in pricing a piece is to have the dealer and the seller each write down a price on paper and then show the paper. This locks the seller into a price. If your offer is higher than the seller's, you pay. But at least the seller can't listen to your offer and then try to jump higher on it. Suppose, for example, the piece in question is a pie safe with fantastic folk art tins. You write down that you will give $200 for it. The owner writes down that he will sell it for $150. You're stuck with paying the higher price, but if you had simply offered him $200 outright, there's a good chance the owner would have asked $250, essentially using your knowledge of the value of the piece against you.

Buying from Suppliers

As a rule, though, price negotiating in people's homes is more straightforward than that, just as it is when you buy from an individual who shows up at your place of business with something to sell. When people come to him, Don first asks the seller's price and then simply makes an offer. Period. Occasionally he may be willing to go a bit higher, but since he tries hard to make fair offers in the first place, his reputation has gotten around and sellers accept what he offers, especially those with whom he's done business before. Don thinks it's important to be able to work this way, without too much haggling over small amounts, because such negotiating takes a lot of time. Some people who come to buy or sell from dealers are willing to spend almost unlimited amounts of time this way; Don would rather be looking for more antiques or making deals with the rest of the sellers who are apt to get backed up at the shop while time is lost dickering with the first one.

Some of the sellers will probably have *finished* antiques. We talked earlier about getting into the business by finding and finishing a piece or two at a time. Conversely, as a buyer, if you can establish a relationship with a few such people, you have a predictable source of good inventory. As such individuals become accustomed to what you want and what you will pay for it, *they* will begin buying for *you,* just as you begin buying for your customers. If they do a lot of that and don't bother with the refinishing, they fall into one other category of people from whom you can buy antiques: pickers.

Pickers

Dealing with pickers isn't for beginners. They want to sell you a whole load, not just a few pieces. And that load almost certainly will contain more that you don't want than it will good pieces. Don didn't work with pickers until he had been in business for about three years. Today, pickers bring in much of Don's merchandise. He works with many on a continuing basis and has had mostly good experiences with them. Occasionally, though, he's been stung. The greatest temptation for a picker, after he's worked with dealers long enough to develop a sense of what things are worth, is to pick up a load of antiques and junk and either keep or sell to another dealer a couple of the best pieces, then unload the rest with the "regular" dealer-purchaser — Don in this case. Don deals with this by simply refusing to buy anything from them for a while to teach them that he is willing to buy the bad to get the good but if they skim off the good, he won't buy at all.

In the past, Don has dealt with pickers who wanted to negotiate the price of each item in the load separately, but that takes huge amounts of time. Now they agree to figure the load, which means Don looks it over and makes an offer on everything at once. You can see why a beginner needs to wait a while before using pickers.

Pin Hookers

In the beginning you could buy from a pin hooker, however. The term "pin hooker" is derived from the language of herding cattle. With animals it meant using a long hook to select certain animals from a herd. In antiques, a pin hooker is a person who buys individual pieces from shops, sales, and auctions, and sells them by the piece to other dealers. For a beginner, buying from such a person can be a good way to pick up merchandise from places you can't visit yourself.

One potential problem with this kind of buying is the occasional dishonest picker or pin hooker or, worse yet, one who has been honest so far, who sells you stolen goods. It happened to Don for the first time just as we were beginning work on this book. He bought an old icebox with no door from a picker he had bought things from before. Because it was late and he was in a hurry, Don broke his own rules and not only paid with cash rather than a check, but also neglected to get a receipt. The story grew long and complicated. We won't spell out everything that happened, but it resulted in the police showing up to question Don, Don learning that the icebox had been stolen from a shed, and Don having to return the icebox. He had already sold it to someone else and, of course, had to refund the money. And he couldn't get back his money for buying the icebox in the first place.

You don't need much imagination to see what it cost him in time, energy, and frustration, as well as money. The lesson in this is that as a buyer you should keep a purchases journal, keep receipts, and pay by check. The IRS likes these rules, too, as we'll explain in the chapter on business affairs. Another lesson is to know your pickers. If the police visit you for such episodes very often, you may be charged with receiving stolen goods. The best defense is to pay honest wholesale prices, which will attract good pickers, and, of course, to keep receipts.

Don has put a lot of effort into developing loyal, honest, dependable suppliers: individuals, pickers, and other dealers. He tries hard to be fair without being a sucker. Sometimes he pays more than he should for things; sometimes he buys items he doesn't really want. If an older person comes in with a few old pieces that really aren't much good and Don knows that the person is depending on selling them for grocery money, he'll buy — even though he doesn't want the goods. In fact, he buys things he doesn't really want quite often because he sees it as part of maintaining relationships with people who come to sell him antiques. Also, he doesn't like to disappoint anybody or hurt their feelings. He says this kind of buying is probably his greatest business weakness, but it has a positive side, too. It earns him loyalty. Often — not always, but often — when someone finds an especially desirable piece or wants to pass on a good bargain, they come first to Don. And since they know he won't quarrel about paying a fair price, they accept what he offers.

Buying is an endless process. Don says, "Sometimes you'd like to stop but you can't because then you're out of business." And since it *is* an on-going process, Don finds that trying to be fair and maintaining a reputation for honesty make it easier and ultimately more profitable than yielding to the temptation to grab a quick cheater's profit when it comes up.

It works the same way with selling, which is obviously the flip side of buying. We'll discuss selling in the following chapter.

CHAPTER 6
How to Sell Antiques

The antiques business differs from other retail businesses in selling just as it does in buying. As we've said, in antiques, buying is the key to success. If you buy well, your merchandise will almost sell itself. In most retail businesses you order stock similar to that carried by your competitors and then look for zingy ways to merchandise it so that people will buy yours instead of theirs. In antiques, having merchandise your competitors couldn't get makes the sale. Don said the other day, "If you had the right merchandise, you could just dump it all in the center of a barn floor and it would sell." Of course not all your merchandise will be that wonderful, no matter how hard you try. And in the antiques business, as in any business, you can learn tricks of merchandising and display that will help your sales. You can learn ways of dealing with customers that will encourage them to come back often. But we must emphasize that although these things will *help along* an antiques business with good merchandise, they simply will not save a business with the wrong goods.

Starting with the assumption that you will be selling desirable merchandise, then, let's look at how you can keep business brisk.

Somewhere, somebody wants everything you've got. The problem is letting them know you have it. There's more involved than advertising. Of course your sign should be as big as you can make it and it should say ANTIQUES in big letters. Those cute, tasteful little signs may be aesthetically pleasing, but people don't always see them. The sign will help pull in new customers. So will ads in antiques publications and the local papers. But getting to know your regular customers and turning sporadic ones into regulars is more important than advertising when it comes to building a profitable business.

You can buy hundreds of books on selling and customer relations. To the degree that their advice applies to *all* selling operations, we don't want to duplicate it. However, we do want to tell you about some practices that are especially important in the antiques business. They have to do with making people feel that being your customer gives them special advantages as antiques buyers.

Dealing with Customers

It starts the first time a customer walks in the door. Lots of people will tell you they're browsing, which is fine, because impulse buying works in the antiques business just as it does at supermarkets, bookstores, and K-Mart. But, without being pushy, you should try to determine the general interests of the new customer. Don usually says, "If you're looking for anything in particular, let me know and I'll point you in the right direction." That lets customers know he won't hang around and high-pressure them, but will help them as much as they want. For some people, being ignored is as bad as being pressured. They get into unfamiliar territory like an antique shop and soon feel overwhelmed by how little they know about what they see. Don tries to alternate periods of browsing time with periods of attention for his customers. He likes to educate new customers about what they're seeing and to be sure those who already *know* what they want can find it.

To work effectively with people who really have come to buy, you need to know what you have in stock, be able to describe it correctly, and help that customer decide if what you have will satisfy his or her needs. Don spends as much time talking people out of buying the wrong pieces as he does selling. Last week, for example, he had a small oak hall tree that had just come in. In the course of a single day he steered three customers away from it, explaining that it was patched in several places and had a seat made of new wood. All three were considering it for their homes. Eventually, Don will either run it through an auction or sell it to an auctioneer. In those situations he doesn't worry about protecting a customer, since, as we've shown, part of the auction game is, "Buyer beware."

Often, if you can't produce what a customer wants immediately, you can watch for it as you're buying and call when you find the right piece.

Buying specifically for customers gives you a good chance of making a sale and guarantees good feeling that you remembered what they like. But, even when you think you're sure a customer wants a particular item, don't buy it unless you're willing to carry it as stock. In other words, don't buy it unless you can handle the possibility that your prospective customer didn't really mean it, has found another source, or has changed his or her mind. Beginning dealers especially get into trouble when they think they know what a customer wants, when, in fact, they haven't got enough information. Suppose someone comes in and says to you, "I'm looking for a meat block."

You put time and energy into finding one and get all excited when you locate one you can buy for $200, figuring to sell it for $300. You muscle its 800 pounds in and out of your truck and into your shop. You call the customer and says, "I've found your meat block. I'll need to get $300 for it."

The response is, "You've gotta be crazy. I wouldn't put a cent over $50 into a meat block."

No sale. If you're lucky, someone else will come in who's willing to pay the price you need for a meat block.

When a customer mentions wanting a specific item, Don usually says, "I get them in. They usually run about $—," and he quotes a price. At that point, the customer's response will give you a good idea of whether or not you should start searching. Even then, Don urges not to buy anything for a customer that you aren't willing to carry as stock. Special deals, even with good friends, do fall through.

Another way you can build a customer base is by letting people know when something comes in that they might want. If you get a very good piece that you know a particular collector will want, you should call or drop a postcard describing it. Many dealers maintain a card file of serious buyers they call about such finds as Aladdin lamps, signed pottery, architecturals, and coin-op machines. With any unusual piece, somebody, somewhere is trying to find it, but it will sit in your shop unsold until the two of you make contact. The more you know (and can remember or write down) about your customers, the more sales you can make.

For less stupendous discoveries, waiting until a regular customer comes in and then just mentioning something new and interesting you have works well, too. It has to be done in such a way that people don't feel pressured to buy something they don't want, however, or they'll stop showing up. For instance, to a customer who has bought iron pieces in the past, Don will just say something like, "Oh, by the way, there's a nice old iron plant stand out front that you might want to look at." Then he lets the matter drop. A customer can pursue it or not without feeling uncomfortable either way.

Letting people browse as long as they like without feeling that you're trying to make them buy something is important. On the other hand, people don't like to be ignored. And if they're making their first timid forays into antiques, they don't want to be intimidated.

Wouldn't you expect it to be obvious? If you want to sell to folks you can't get far by being mean and hateful and obnoxious. But just thinking about your own trips to antiques shops will tell you that a surprising number of people trying to run antiques businesses either don't understand the obvious or can't practice what they know. Every buyer just learning about antiques can tell stories about dealers who made them feel stupid — not just unlearned in antiques, but *stupid*. And way too many of us can tell stories about being assured that we were about to buy an antique worth its price tag only to learn later that it was a reproduction or a "married" or patched piece. A "married" piece is one that has been put together or reconstructed from the parts of two or more broken or incomplete items.

A determined customer may put up with your bad disposition or half-truths once or twice, but an antiques business depends strongly on repeat customers and only those few looking for punishment will return consistently to a place of business where they feel badly treated or ignored.

Grace Under Pressure

If you're nodding and thinking, "Well, certainly, I'll be pleasant to my customers," let us show you that it's not always as easy as it sounds. For one thing, if you have a shop, especially a successful one, you'll rarely have the luxury of focusing on one customer at a time, flashing your smile and proffering your advice. Someone will be trying to sell you antiques at the same time you're trying to deal with your own customers. Serious customers will get mixed in with people entertaining themselves on a dull afternoon who ask two hours' worth of questions and end up spending $2. If you specialize in glass, count on a fair share of mommies with wild kids darting around. If you are proud of selling nicely finished tables, expect some joker to leave his initials on one. If you are building your reputation on selling only authentic pieces, watch for the inevitable know-it-all who says loudly that your finest piece is really a reproduction. Set your mind to deal with the cheapskate who tries to force you lower on an already very low price.

Don is an easy-going person with a genuine tolerance for all kinds of people, but even he admits to getting testy at the end of a bad day. Nobody understands better than Don that the annoyances typical of the business must not keep you from working with all new customers to make them feel that being a customer of yours offers special advantages.

Last week, a young couple with a small boy and a week-old infant came to Don's shop on a very busy day. The father sat in the car with the baby, while his little boy and wife wandered through the barns. When Don was free to give her some attention, she said, "I need a little chest about this high to put at the end of a hall. I don't know anything about antiques or anything, but could you suggest something?"

Don showed her several chests and told her the prices. Her attention was diverted by the oak hall tree we told you about earlier in this chapter. "That's pretty. How much is it?" she said.

"It's a hundred and a quarter, but I don't recommend it," Don said. "It's patched in several places, and the seat is all new wood."

She wandered off, browsing idly while her son poked in corners.

Another customer came to pick up a door Don had been saving for him.

The woman came back to ask the price on a couple more items, including a pine table sitting outside. "I'm afraid it's pretty expensive," Don said.

When she heard the price, the woman visibly lost interest in the table, but eventually she got her husband to come in and look at a chest. And she said, oh, incidentally, her son liked that toy wood airplane back in the corner, how much was that? Don said he was afraid it was pretty expensive, too, because it was an early handmade toy. It was about $100. The woman visibly lost interest again.

The telephone rang three different times. Don sat in his old barber chair to talk. He asked one person to call back later, made an appointment to have the next caller bring him a truckload, and told the third that he didn't have what she wanted right now but might after the truckload came in — check back on Friday.

The little family who didn't know anything about antiques asked the prices on a couple more pieces and wandered away. On the way out they passed a pregnant woman coming in saying pretty much the same things they had said, except that she needed a nice little table for her bedroom.

Later the family returned and bought a chest for $50. Not a huge purchase, perhaps, but it could be the first of many. If they become seriously interested in antiques, they'll know and trust Don because he was careful to be fair and honest. Even though he was very busy, he found time to pay attention to them. And no matter how silly their questions sounded, he did not make them feel stupid for asking. Even if they don't get into antiques in a big way, they're going to need lots more chests and tables and chairs as the kids grow. Smaller purchases add up, and on a day when nothing else has happened, $50 looks good. To repeat an important point illustrated by this story: pay attention to all your customers. In a business as much like a huge club as antiques, it's easy to get into the habit of chatting with your regulars and ignoring unfamiliar customers, especially if they don't look like serious buyers. It's a habit that could put you out of business. To survive, you need to hold on to the idea that everybody who comes through the door of your shop is somebody you might be able to sell something to.

When you're very busy, you'll sometimes have to decide who gets your attention first. Sometimes the choices should be obvious after you learn the buying habits of your regulars. For instance, there's one dealer who buys regularly from Don. When he shows up, Don gets to him immediately and sticks to him like glue until he's gone, because in twenty minutes he can buy several thousand dollars' worth of merchandise. Don knows him to be a buyer who knows what he wants, understands its value, and comes intent on buying.

You can expect at least three different kinds of customers: those who know what they're doing, those who don't know and admit it, and those who don't know what they're doing but think they do. Each needs to be handled differently. The knowledgeable buyers will probably be your best customers and, when you have to choose, should receive the greater part of your attention. But people who don't know about antiques buy them, too. Sometimes a customer who doesn't know antiques will begin with you by purchasing one piece and will return, gradually learning more, and eventually becoming a good customer.

Attracting Business

Clearly, it's to your advantage to be polite, helpful, *and* honest. A few days ago, a Cadillac full of silver-haired ladies stopped at Cline's "just to look" on a day when the barns are typically closed. As they left, thanking Don for letting them in, they asked about some pitchers they had seen inside. Don told them that at least one of the pitchers had a cracked spout. After they'd gone, he repeated his familiar line that such honesty "isn't just Christian charity." Not only does it help build his reputation as a reliable dealer who can be trusted by customers who need expert help, but also it keeps people from buying things, discovering flaws at home, and returning the damaged goods. This is all part of making customers feel that it is to their advantage to buy antiques from you.

The Value of Specialties

Another way to attract customers is by publicizing your specialties. Perhaps it would be more accurate to say that *having* specialties attracts customers. We don't mean to suggest that you have to do a lot of costly advertising. Word-of-mouth does a lot for you. So does handing out business cards with information about the areas in which you specialize. Don's card, for example, lists primitives, oak, country-store items, advertising, woodstoves, pottery, and tools. You probably wouldn't have so many different specialties in the beginning, but even if you had only one or two, a business card would be effective. Non-competing dealers and gift shop proprietors often will let you leave cards in their stores, and of course you can hand them out generously at flea markets, auctions, and anywhere else potential customers gather.

Keep Merchandise Moving

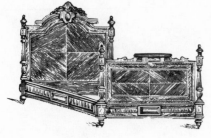

Don's card also mentions constantly changing merchandise. Whether you have one specialty or many, keeping new items coming into the shop all the time is one of the best traffic builders in the business. We've mentioned it several times but it bears repeating. Some dealers go so far as to hold back part of loads they buy to feed them into the shop gradually. It works because so many antiques hunters keep at it all the time. Of course, some people decide they need a bed or a chest and go to an antiques shop to buy it and then don't come back for six months or longer, until they need something else. But far more people amuse themselves in their leisure time by watching for desirable pieces. If they learn that your shop has pretty much the same stuff in it week after week, they'll soon get bored and stop coming. But if they know that you'll have new things every week, they'll show up that often. The same is true of other people who, like you, are buying and selling antiques as a business. You may be picking shops looking for your specialty; others will pick your shop for the same reason. Fine. A customer is a customer; a sale is a sale. Better to have a picker come in and buy things once a week than once every six months.

How to Increase Traffic

This brings us to a way of luring people into your shop even when they're not necessarily planning to buy anything. You can offer a related service. One dealer in our area specializes in stripping and refinishing. Like Don, she has a country location, but not the space or other resources to operate on as large a scale as he does. Many of her customers buy antiques elsewhere and bring them to her to be finished. The back part of her shop is full of such pieces, none of them for sale. But in front she has a small but regularly changing assortment of chairs, chests, trunks, and so on that are for sale. (Some of them she has bought from Don.) A customer unloading a table to be stripped or refinished may very well see a couple of nice chairs and buy them before leaving.

Elsewhere in our locality, an in-town dealer specializes in woodworking and repair. We call him a wood magician. Suppose you've bought a nice old pie safe that has part of its back or side missing. With his furniture building skills, he can fix it, drawing on his stock of old wood, so that the repair hardly shows. His work area is in the back of a large shop. Two other rooms, including a big display window on the sidewalk side, are filled with antiques, many refinished, for sale. They are arranged in groupings like room settings to attract maximum attention. You come in to get your pie safe repaired and go out having bought an oak rocker or a brass lantern or a silver dresser set. The wood magician also sells refinishing supplies, books about antiques, some nonantique gift shop items, and a few reproductions. He says the small gift items not only sell well to customers interested in antiques, but when they are displayed with antiques in his big window, also attract passersby into the shop.

The service you offer should depend on what you enjoy about antiques. If you hate refinishing or are allergic to the chemicals in stripping tanks, you can't offer those services as part of your business. If you can't repair broken things, that's not an option either, unless you decide to hire someone part-time to do it for you. But your own interests, which influence your specialties, will also help you shape related services to attract customers. We offer some examples to stimulate your imagination.

- Offer decorating services to people who like antiques but don't know how to incorporate them into their homes.
- Teach classes in your shop about your specialties—furniture of particular periods, art, glass, etc.
- Establish a lending library of books related to antiques.
- Specialize in patching and repair work; leave the refinishing and chemicals to someone else.
- Offer picture framing for old artwork and advertising signs and labels.
- Supply parts for antique automobiles.

- Sell items related to radios, phonographs, and juke boxes: records, vacuum tubes, small light bulbs, etc. Or repair these pieces of equipment.
- Restore wicker furniture. Teach classes in repairing wicker and basket weaving.
- Cane chairs. Teach classes in chair caning.
- Open a doll hospital for antique dolls. Make authentic reproduction costumes for dolls.
- Devote a large part of your stock to all kinds of antique toys.
- Publish a newsletter about your specialty. (For example, the newsletter *Tags 'n' Stuff* about license plates, circulates to about 2,000 readers. It carries classifieds for people who want to buy and sell old license plates.)
- Collect and sell all the items related to railroad travel: timetables, lanterns, locks, keys, tools, dining car china, etc. Or narrow the field still more and become an expert in just one of those things.

Develop any interest or service or specialty that will fit the way you like to spend your time and will attract more customers into your shop.

Your Own Style

By now you should begin to see some emerging patterns. Regardless of what we tell you, your own selling style is going to reflect your personality. If you're an aggressive person, you'll probably sell aggressively. If you're shy, you may have trouble talking to your customers. You certainly won't get into hard sell.

Similarly, what you sell in your shop and to whom you sell it is inextricably bound up with your choices in display and merchandising. The kinds of things you sell and the location from which you do it will give you ideas about how to display and merchandise your goods. Let's consider Don's operation as an example.

In many ways, it is not a typical situation. Don wholesales much more than most dealers. He is geared to rapid turnover of large pieces, especially rough country items. He has room for big old advertising signs, decorative woodwork from demolished old houses, iron work, big furniture pieces, and even an occasional jukebox. Goods come and go by the truckload. If you see something you like on Tuesday and don't buy it, you can expect it to be gone by Wednesday.

The operation suits people who want to buy in volume. It appeals to those who want to buy rough and refinish. It's fun for folks who like to browse through mountains of merchandise looking for special surprises. But it's not the ideal *retail* setup, and it's not suited to selling fine china or glass. Although a few dainty things pass through from time to time, few customers who go to Cline's are looking for them. The setup won't appeal to anyone who hates getting dirty hands. It won't work easily for people who have to have everything arranged in room-like settings before they can visualize what a piece will be like in their own homes. It's not much of a place to find a $15 gift that you can take right home and wrap.

Down the road from Cline's is a little shop full of refinished furniture, glassware, silver, and oil lamps. The place is crowded, but the dresser sets are arranged on dressers; lamps are on tables; bookends are displayed with books. Prices are higher. Customers who buy there rarely if ever go to Cline's. The shop specializes, among other things, in oil lamps. You'd have a hard time buying an oil lamp at Cline's because every week or so that shop owner stops in and buys any that Don has acquired, taking them back, polishing them up, and fitting them in nicely with the rest of his cleaned-up merchandise. His shop is always busy. Clearly, many customers like this kind of merchandising. It suits them and it suits the dealer.

Both shops are in country locations, but where Cline's is down a dirt lane on a farm, the other shop is right alongside the road in a more upscale community, an ideal location for a fancy shop.

Display

Another common and successful approach to merchandising is to have one area set up as a display center for some of your cleaner pieces, while maintaining the rest of your space for a more rough-and-tumble approach. The nicely finished and displayed pieces will necessarily be more expensive, but you can use them to show customers how similar, unrefinished pieces in your stock will look. This is especially effective with a clientele in which some customers can afford fancy prices but most others can't.

As a lover of constant turnover, Don has a personal prejudice against displays that are too polished and pretty. He says they make him suspicious because he wonders how come the dealer has all that time to spend dusting things. But he'd be the first to agree that there are customers for that look, too.

If you like antiques, no doubt you've seen lots of merchandising options yourself. You've seen entire houses furnished with antiques room-by-room. And you've seen entire houses in which antiques were loaded into rooms but with no effort to display them. Sara used to buy occasionally from a shop in Pennsylvania that had enough rooms to have one for bottles and glass, another for chairs, another for books, in a dizzying number of rooms. The house had a front and back staircase and three full stories of antiques and junk. It was the kind of place that left you feeling you could go into the house some Saturday morning and disappear forever. Sadly, the shop didn't do as well as it should have, given the quality of what was in it, because many customers were intimidated by all those cluttered little rooms. Many similar items sold better and at higher prices in a tidy little

gift shop in the same town, where a few choice antiques were included as a sideline along with dried flowers, candles, and perfumed soaps.

You Have to Choose

The way you choose to merchandise isn't as important as the fact of choosing. You can probably make almost anything work if you've made a deliberate choice and set about implementing it. For instance, Don and Vikki recently decided too much clutter had accumulated around the front of the main barns. They thought they were losing customers who were put off by the piles of junk they encountered before they got to where the good antiques were. Don had some salable items, such as pieces of old iron, hauled back to a field where they didn't show. Lots of junk he just had hauled to the dump. Hard-to-handle items such as the big cigarette signs were stacked neatly along the wall. Inside, he got rid of much of the purely worthless stuff that had accumulated as the result of buying whole loads just to get the few good things in them. To the casual observer, little has changed. But, in fact, Don has cleared out the junk so that it is possible for a customer to get to the antiques more easily without sacrificing the sense of browsing for bargains.

Don also thinks it's important to display similar kinds of antiques together and to take full advantage of your location. A good primitive country piece appeals to a knowledgeable buyer and also to less aware customers if they see it in the context of other country pieces. But if that same piece were next to a fine walnut Victorian chest or in a room full of glossy mahogany or cherry furniture, it would look crude and inappropriate. People love to buy primitives out of a barn. They will dig for them because they like the feeling that they're discovering them for the first time. People like to think that everything they find in your country barn used to belong to your neighbors. The same primitive pieces might not sell as well in an expensive uptown location. The opposite is also true. The expensive Oriental pieces you see in city shops don't seem appropriate to out-of-the-way sheds surrounded by woods and fields. Moreover, the people who like such furniture generally wouldn't be interested in rooting through a barn to find it.

The Retailer's Approach

The more heavily oriented your shop is toward retail business, the more important display becomes. You should group or cluster items in some consistent way so that you and your customers know where to find them. You might put all the clocks on one place, all the dolls in another, and so on. Then, customers searching for specialties know where in your shop to look for any new clocks or dolls.

Retailers arrange displays according to one of two opposing principles. The first is to assemble a lot of the same or similar mer-

chandise in one place for impact. This is the same principle you see applied when a bookstore, for instance, fills an entire table with many copies of the same title. In antiques, you might assemble all the lamps or quilts or depression glass this way, to attract attention. The other approach is to scatter the pieces around, make them look scarce. If you have, say, ten clocks, you might put out only five of them and not all in the same place. The reasoning behind this approach is that too many choices actually befuddle shoppers, paralyzing them with indecision so that they end up buying nothing at all. We believe the first approach is the better one, but what *you* believe is more important. The method that you think is best is the method that will work best for you.

In showing furniture, you should try to display it as it is used as much as space permits. Beds sell better if customers see them assembled. Dining sets sell better if the chairs are arranged around the table and the sideboard is in an appropriate place. Some dealers will go so far as to set the table with antique dishes and silver, but such a display takes time and has to be changed every time you sell something — which should be often. Basically, knowing that good antiques *will* sell themselves and knowing, also, that effective merchandising and display may help sell them faster and for a better price, you should do as much as you have time for and feel comfortable with.

Competing for Flea Market Sales

So far, we have been talking about selling from a shop. When you're selling at flea markets, the rules change quite a bit. For one thing, you don't have the same need to build relationships with repeat customers. You can certainly build a clientele through flea market activity, but many of your sales will be one-shots, and as with auctions, the bargain-hunting mentality predominates. Don would be as honest about the condition of his antiques at a flea market as he is in his shop, but he probably wouldn't work as hard to talk people out of buying pieces he doesn't think will suit them later.

Moreover, because of the competition and traffic at flea markets, having a strong display isn't just nice, it is absolutely critical. When you realize that you may have one of a thousand booths at a large flea market and that people will be wandering up and down the aisles only about half focused until something catches their eyes, you see why it is a hard-sell situation.

If you're not the used-car salesman type at heart, you will need a knockout display to attract attention. As always, having good merchandise works. Showing a very good piece, even if it is expensive, will do it. So will putting out bright quilts or colorful rugs or a row of eye-catching old toys. One of the most successful flea market displays Don has ever seen was also one of the most outrageous. The booth was dominated by an eight-foot-tall cedar snag — a piece of

tree trunk with bare branches jutting out. The "tree" was laden with scores of Taiwan-made wooden apples. People bought them in huge quantities at about three times their actual cost because the display was so striking.

Think of your flea market booth as theater and your selling activities as your performance. That attitude should keep you competitive.

Ultimately, whether you sell in a flea market or a shop or both, your location, your specialties, and your personality will define a merchandising strategy for you. As long as you haven't copied a dozen other shops or booths in the same three-mile radius with you, you'll find your market niche naturally and develop your customers accordingly.

Pricing – Problems and Strategy

Pricing antiques differs completely from pricing standard merchandise, even new furniture. You can't start with the manufacturer's recommended retail. You can't take the standard wholesale price and simply tag on a percentage markup, because there is no standard wholesale price for antiques. You can't even use a standard percentage markup over what you actually paid for a piece. Beginners often make this mistake.

Don talked recently with a woman who was still new to the business. She had lucked out in buying a sixteen-pane pine corner cupboard for $200. The retail value of the cupboard was about $1,500, but she sold it for only $400. She said, "I just didn't feel right about taking a lot more because I'd paid so little for it." At first you can see why she might feel that way. Looking closer at the way the business works, though, you begin to see that it takes the occasional huge profit on one piece to make up for the slim profit on lots of others and to help pay for the losses you sustain on some of your mistakes.

As an economist, Don would point out that the goal of all companies in business is to make a profit. As an antiques dealer, he'd say you have to hit an occasional lick to stay in business.

Some pieces, such as standard oak furniture, have a fairly standard price. You can find lots of it around; it's factory made; the pieces are pretty much interchangeable. Retail customers expect to pay about $125 for an oak washstand. Pickers, dealers, and even casual traders would expect a wholesale price somewhere between $40 and $65, depending on the condition of the washstand. It's unlikely that you'll find one for $5 to resell.

But a unique piece, especially handmade, one that's unfamiliar to many people, may come to you cheap and be salable for a great deal. You'll learn to recognize such chances to hit a lick as you work and read in the business. Then you'll have to teach yourself to be unashamed of taking the profit when the opportunities come along. Don tries to set fair prices based on a balance between market value and the cost of a piece to him. And he hopes to sneak in a big gain occasionally.

Strangely enough, customers who don't know the true value of antiques probably will make pricing harder for you than those who know what they're doing. Suppose you have a customer who has set aside $500 to buy a nice chest and has decided it should be an antique. It happens that you practically stole one at a yard sale last week and have it priced at $200. But your customer wants a $500 chest. A person like this will very likely go down the road to your competitor, find a less good chest priced at $500 — and buy it. It happens a lot. Not knowing antiques and probably not trusting dealers, such buyers fall back on the old you-get-what-you-pay-for rule. They think that because a piece has a high price tag it must be valuable.

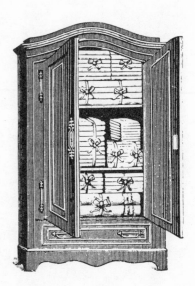

The way your stock moves should be a guide to how well you are pricing things. We said before, if you are sold out before you can even get your booth set up at a flea market, you're too cheap. If you have the same pieces around so long they start to seem like members of the family, you're probably asking too much.

Although you want to get as much as you can for what you sell, pricing too high can hurt you. Don often talks about dealers who try to "extract the max" on every piece they buy and sell. It takes longer for most pieces to sell this way. Not only do you have to be very sure of what the maximum price you can get is, unless you want it around forever, you have to wait until someone willing to pay it shows up. It's a business style directly opposite to the way Don likes to operate. He prefers to turn lots of merchandise at smaller markups, knowing full well that sometimes he doesn't get as much as he could if he waited. Generally, dealers who do business this way make more money than those who try to extract the max, because they sell in greater volume. However, in a classy shop with a good upscale location and elaborate merchandising, it is possible to sell antiques at higher markups and still do a brisk, profitable business. (But don't forget, if your location costs you more, your prices have to be higher to compensate, so you may not be making any more actual profit than a less well-located competitor selling the same kinds of antiques for less.)

About Bargaining

As for customers who like to haggle over all prices, even those already low, you'll have to decide how you want to handle them. Don doesn't often put a price sticker on his merchandise because it moves too fast, but when he does have a posted price, he usually will come down a little if he's asked. But once he's given a price, orally, he won't dicker any more, unless it's something he wants to get rid of badly. Regular customers have come to expect him to make the lowest price he feels he can. They know he won't change it. Most don't ask him to. But some dealers in our area and elsewhere, routinely price their merchandise with a margin for bargaining built in. If a customer quietly pays the first asking price, it's a little gravy. Otherwise, the dealer can come down some when asked and leave customers feeling good about having made a deal.

To give you an idea how silly bargaining can get, Don remembers dealing with a woman who had a small shop and didn't know what she wanted except that she wanted it cheap. She was the kind of buyer who looks at $2,000 worth of merchandise only to spend $100. She came across a pretty matted western print still marked with a flea market tag at $1. She looked at the dollar tag and said, "Is that your best price?"

To his credit, Don resisted the temptation to say, "Do you want me to *pay* you to take it?" She's still an occasional customer.

As we've mentioned, some customers expect to negotiate the prices on everything they buy; others prefer the direct approach. It's all a matter of style, yours and theirs. As the dealer with a shop or flea market booth to run, it's *your* style that should set the tone.

If you are inclined to be devious, Don has decided over the years that one of the best styles for selling lots of merchandise, good and bad, at the highest possible prices, is to act dumb. His professional pride won't let him do it, but he's seen many traders get tremendous mileage out of saying essentially, "I don't know nothin' about this stuff. Here it is and if you want it, this is how much it costs." Many customers walk out of such situations (especially in country locations) carrying expensive junk and feeling superior because they've "really taken a dumb country trader." The funny thing is, such a pose doesn't seem to turn off knowledgeable buyers; it amuses them. We can't advocate it, in good conscience, but if you're going to be in the business, you need to know it's one way some traders sell.

Try All the Markets

One more thing about selling that all sucessful dealers learn is to use all the market possibilities available to keep merchandise moving. If you have a piece that won't sell in your shop, even at a good price, take it to a flea market. If you can't sell it there, try an auctioneer or another dealer, Or, illogical as it sounds, put it away for a while, then get it out again and *raise* the price. Sometimes it works.

Avoid "Keepitis"

We've concentrated so much on telling you how to sell, that we have neglected an important point — that if you're going to be in business, you *must sell.* You'll remember, we mentioned the dangers of "keepitis." Collectors who go into business, or try to, are most apt to find that they just can't bear to part with the good things that come their way.

Suppose you're a collector of antique quilts and you acquire an Amish quilt pieced in the 1930s, in remarkably good condition, and finely quilted with perfectly even stitches. You found it at an out-of-the-way country sale on a rainy day where you bought it for $100. You know you can sell it for at least five times that — a great profit. But it's better than any quilt in your personal collection. How can you give it up? You just have to keep it. If that only happens once, you're okay, especially if you decide to sell some other quilt from your collection instead. But what about the next perfect example of quilting that you find?

If you can afford to keep it, great! Some dealers are basically collectors who buy some items for resale but keep everything in their collecting fields. They may expect to put all their profits back into their collections. But most of us have to sell in order to eat.

Don knows many collectors who opened shops and thus had the excuse to attend many more auctions and pick many more other shops, all in the name of business. Naturally, they found so much they wanted to keep that they spent all their operating capital or "trading money" on items they couldn't bring themselves to sell. The merchandise may accrue in value enough to make money for them, or their heirs, someday, but that is not certain. If you look at the compound interest the same amount of money could have earned if invested, you'll find that often keeping too much actually costs money. Also, it puts your shop out of business. The best defense against keepitis for collectors is to specialize in selling something that you are genuinely interested in and like, but don't collect passionately. Probably it's not a good idea to try to sell things that don't interest you at all. You'll do it badly.

Some dealers who aren't collectors have trouble selling choice pieces because they like to keep them around to study, research the price, and maybe work on them a little before letting them go to a customer. Don says such people fool with their antiques so long, they wear them out. Probably the best solution to that inclination is to have merchandise coming in so regularly that you must keep inventory moving out.

Sometimes you'll get your hands on a piece so rare or unusual (or simply unfamiliar to you) that you either have no sure idea what it's worth or you want to take the time to get top dollar from someone who appreciates its value. In this case, you really do need to hold on to it for a while. *The worst thing you can do is leave it in your shop.* Nothing frustrates people more than admiring something and then being told it's not for sale. Don gets damned mad when people keep stuff in their shop and won't sell. So do other customers. Instead, put it in your house. Dealers commonly keep some choice pieces in their homes, occasionally moving them out and replacing them with others. It's understood in the business that if you have something good in your house, you'll mention it in a low-key way to potential buyers.

Recently Don bought an old hunt board in a load brought to him by a picker. Knowing that it was rare and could bring a very high price, Don turned down an on-the-spot offer for $1,000, saying that

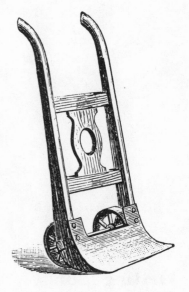

he was going to take it home because it was just the right height to put his television on in the bedroom — the way the television had been placed put a crick in his neck. Well, it's hard to find something the right height for watching television from bed, and now that he'd found it in the hunt board, Don let it be known it wasn't for sale.

Except, of course, it is for sale — at the right price. And in time Don will say to the right prospect, "Oh, by the way, I've got an old pine southern hunt board over at the house that you might be interested in." And then Don will have to find something else to keep his television on. Until then, he's watching television comfortably, the piece is out of sight of customers who can't or wouldn't pay the price, and even though it's serving as furniture in the Cline household, it's accruing in value. It is possible that no one will ever be willing to pay the price or that people interested in old hunt boards will suddenly disappear from the face of the earth. Don would never take home such an expensive piece unless he was willing to keep it forever, if that's how things should work out.

This is the accepted way of handling an occasional exceptional piece, but you can see how easily it could turn into another version of "keepitis" and you'd end up with more of your stock at home than in your shop. You just can't get too attached to anything. Antiques dealers joke about feeling like strangers in their own homes because they keep changing the furniture there. The point is that bringing pieces home can be a good idea, as long as you eventually sell them out and as long as you allow for the possibility that you won't get any more offers as high as those you've already passed up.

A curious flip side to all this is that sometimes you sell the same piece over and over and just can't get rid of it. Don has seen an oak kitchen clock, the kind commonly called a "roosterhead," pass through his shop at least five times. In fact, he remembers selling the same clock to the same clock dealer for the same price five times. It got to be a joke between them. It happens for all kinds of reasons. People who trade in antiques actually constitute a pretty small club. Someone who buys the piece may sell it at a markup to another dealer. That dealer may get in a jam and need money. He'll haul a load to someone like Don for quick cash and in buying the load, Don may get the piece back for much less than his original selling price. If you can keep track of what you've sold it for, you may make a little extra money.

Getting Your Money

So far we have talked mainly about *how* to sell antiques. We should turn our attention, at least briefly, to how to make sure the transaction really is a sale and not a give-away. It's appallingly easy to end up giving away your antiques if you're not careful. Don has learned that you'll always be able to find people who are willing to separate you from your merchandise. Someone always wants what you have.

Getting them to pay you money for it is more complicated. The two areas in which you're most apt to run into trouble are accepting personal checks and being asked to extend credit.

Checks

You should know the following about checks. If you accept out-of-state checks that bounce, you might as well consider the money gone. Although some states have agreements with bordering states to the contrary, most states will not serve warrants for out-of-state checks.

Local checks are less risky, but even then con artists find ways to get your antiques without paying you for them. Dealers in our area all know a woman who used to buy antiques and pay for them with unsigned checks. She managed it by being cute, charming, and chatty while she wrote and handed over the checks for what she bought. In the ensuing good humor and the confusion of loading, the dealers stuck the checks in their pockets or cash drawers without looking closely at them. When they noticed the missing signature, they'd contact the charming crook. She would refuse to sign or make good on the check. Legally the dealers hadn't any recourse. The check was worthless because it was unsigned, but they had accepted it that way. The fact that they didn't know it was worthless didn't pertain because, technically, it was perfectly obvious. There's no allowance in business law for carelessness. Of course, it didn't take long for word to get around, and once it had no one would deal with her on anything but a cash basis.

You can be taken if you accept post-dated checks, too. They're illegal. If you make a sale on June 1, agree to accept and hold a check for it dated June 5, and the check bounces even though you wait to cash it, you can't prosecute. If you do occasionally agree to hold a check for someone, make sure that it is dated for the day of the sale.

When a check you deposit from someone you trust bounces, you may want to redeposit it and see if it's good the second time. Sometimes when people buy things like antiques, they transfer money from one account to another to cover the checks they write. Don't expect too much success, though. Most banks automatically process a check a second time if it showed insufficient funds, but redepositing a check has become common practice for many businesses. Of course, these days, many banks charge you a fee for processing an insufficient-funds check, no matter whether you wrote it or deposited it. The nature of your relationship with the customer, the size of the check in relationship to the size of the fee, and the amount of business you hope to do with that person in the future will all be factors in how you handle it. On the one hand, you'd hate to lose $5,000 worth of business trying to collect a $5 service charge. On the other hand, you're losing money if you have to pay a $10 service charge on a $15 check. When you think about the problems that go with accepting checks, you may be tempted to work on a cash-only basis, but as anybody knows who has tried to use cash to rent a car or a hotel room lately, we don't live in a cash society any more. Not accepting checks will probably cost you more in loss of business than you'll save in bad checks. Look at each check carefully, get full information on address and telephone on each one, and try to develop some instincts for the kinds of people who are most apt to pass you bad checks. As we said earlier, you can't tell much from the way people dress or the vehicles they drive. Accepting checks from your repeat customers, your regulars, certainly constitutes the lowest risk.

Credit

Extending credit is a risk you don't have to take at all. Don urges that you never let anyone take a piece away without paying you. And, as he says, sooner or later a situation will come up when you do it anyway. Customers generally do not expect credit when buying antiques, so you probably won't lose business by not extending it. Don occasionally does work on credit with someone and almost always ends up wishing he hadn't. He does it because he's too soft, not because it's good business. So much of his business is wholesale to other dealers, at a small margin of profit, that he can't afford to accept credit cards. (Banks levy a service fee, a percentage of sales, against the seller.) However, in a mostly retail shop, especially in an area where much of your business is from tourists, you may eventually decide it is worth the bank charge to be able to accept credit cards. In fact, some dealers who refuse checks accept credit cards. If you want to do this, contact several banks and talk to them about opening a merchant account. Consult with the bank where you now do business about adding credit cards to your services. The terms differ from bank to bank, so don't just accept the first one you hear from. Most of them will charge a one-time opening fee, a small rental on the credit card imprinting machine, and a percentage (usually about 3 percent) of your credit card sales. In a situation where you sell to many people you don't know, the credit card services would probably be worth the cost in the long run.

Layaway

Another problem you sometimes encounter in selling antiques is customers who ask you to hold merchandise for them. We can list as many reasons as you have customers — short of cash, no place to put the piece, no way to haul it home, have to check with a spouse or associate first, need to measure a space to see if it will fit — maybe you've even made a few such requests yourself. It is poor business to hold merchandise for one customer if you've got another customer, with the money, ready to buy on the spot. But sometimes you'll no doubt do it. And, you'll probably wish you hadn't. Sometimes customers change their minds and never come back, even if they've put down a deposit. It's hard to understand why people do it, but Don has become convinced over the years that certain shoppers see antiques they can't afford, but they want them anyway. Either they are embarrassed to admit they can't afford them, or they are embarrassed to leave without buying anything, or they kid themselves into believing they'll find a way to come up with the money. You may pass up good offers on the items meantime. Once a customer gave Don a $10 deposit on a wood cookstove and came back five years later to get it. He was upset that it was gone. Even so, Don was generous about it. He tripped over that stove daily for two years before he got disgusted and sold it. If you are going to hold something for a customer, ask for a significant deposit and make it clear how long you will wait before considering the piece for sale again if it's not picked up. Usually, such a deposit is not refunded if the customer changes his mind, though some dealers will make allowances (agreed upon ahead of time) for regular customers.

Returns

One last problem we need to mention is returned merchandise. You can avoid many returns just by making sure customers know what's wrong with a piece when they buy it. If you point out the chipped veneer, broken leg, or cracked lid at the time of purchase, customers can't bring back the dresser or chair or candy dish because of the chip, break, or crack. But some returners are more devious. A dealer may buy something from you and want to return it when it doesn't sell in a few weeks. Or a collector may pick up an expensive piece and then, when other bills start piling up, decide it was a mistake to spend the money. Or a husband buys it for his wife and she hates it. Decorators often like to take a piece and try it out to see how it works. Don's policy is to take back a piece and give the customer credit toward buying something else, or sometimes to buy back the piece at what he originally paid for it, but not at what the customer paid him. Sometimes people ask to return for more legitimate reasons. Recently, for example, a woman bought a chest of drawers to repair and finish. She knew what was wrong with it. When her husband took out the drawers, he said he wasn't capable of fixing them himself. In that case, Don took back the chest and returned the money. Except in such rare instances, it is poor business practice in antiques to give cash refunds when someone wants to return something. Sometimes, though, to close a sale, Don will say to a customer, "Take it home and try it. If it doesn't work, bring it back." But he doesn't do that often and he never makes the offer unless he really is willing to get the piece back and refund the money.

Perhaps you're wondering if it isn't contradictory for us to refer to good business practices and, in the next sentence, talk about times when you might make an exception to your rules. Clearly, it would be easiest and safest *never* to hold a check, *never* to extend credit, *never* to keep merchandise without a deposit, and *never* to

make cash refunds for returns. Why should you make any exceptions at all? Because sometimes you'll feel mean and nasty if you don't. Sometimes you'll ruin what has been a valuable working relationship with someone. Don says, "Not all people who deal in antiques are flakes, but being a little weird helps." It follows that being a little weird will create situations in which "standard business practices" seem inappropriate. Indeed, Don says, "The antiques business attracts a lot of unusual people who are refugees from the respectable business world. Antiques types reject standard business practices."

Staying in the antiques business, then, requires more flexibility than you might need in some other kinds of business. But it also requires a willingness to practice conscientiously and consistently those "standard business practices," even if you do it in a way uniquely your own. One of the hardest parts of starting something like an antiques business is learning to treat its elements in a businesslike manner rather than as a hobby.

According to figures from the Small Business Administration, 90 percent of all new businesses fail. The failures are caused mainly by *business* incompetence. This contributes to the mystique that business is complicated and requires esoteric knowledge about such mysteries as double-entry bookkeeping. In fact, good business practice is not complicated. Mainly, it requires daily record keeping. For some of us, it would be easier to learn something complicated than it is to learn to write down everything. But if you don't keep records, you can't even be sure whether you're making or losing money — until the bank tells you, and then it's too late. The following chapter is about the basics of small business practice, especially as they apply to beginners. Nothing we've said in any of the preceding chapters will do you much good in starting a successful antiques business unless you grit your teeth and *do* what we describe in our chapter about business fundamentals.

CHAPTER 7

Taking Care of Business

To be successful, you cannot run an antiques business as though it were a hobby. This means doing some things you probably don't like to do: keeping records, separating your personal income from your business income, filling out forms, and paying taxes. There is a tremendous temptation in the antiques business just to let money fall between the cracks. People often pay in cash. The value of pieces fluctuates, so who's to know what your inventory is worth? You sell a piece, slip the cash into your pocket, and later in the day spend it on something you've been wanting. Some business experts say that most small businesses operate illegally and that many antiques dealers participate in this underground economy. Don doesn't. Neither should you.

The first reason is simple. If caught, you can be prosecuted for fraud and, if convicted, fined and sent to jail. Also, if you are successful with antiques you could eventually end up making more money than you can hide, which brings us back to fraud and jail. A third reason to keep your operation above board from the beginning is that you'll actually be better off financially taking advantage of the legitimate deductions and discounts that are part of an honest business, than you would be trying to get by illegally. In the antiques business, you can deduct from your taxable income such expenses as traveling to shows, the cost of a vehicle to haul antiques in, and subscriptions to periodicals. Since you'd probably incur these expenses whether you are in business or not, it's like getting deductions for your hobby. Except, as we said, you cannot behave as though you are indulging in a hobby.

Honesty Pays

Not a Hobby

The most important difference between a business and a hobby in antiques is that a business requires you to write down everything related to it — every cent you spend, every item you buy, every piece you sell, every dollar you earn. When you listen to accountants talk, it sounds complicated. Most of us are intimidated by conversations full of "single entry ledgers," "P & L analysis," and "cash accounting." But it's only the language, not its meaning, that is intimidating. Single entry just means that you only have to write down income or expenditures once to keep track of them. P & L analysis is figuring out whether you had a profit or a loss. Cash accounting means you write down income when you get it and expenses when you pay them. We'll go into more detail about how to do this when we get to our discussion on setting up and keeping books. At this point, all we want to do is emphasize that you're going to have to do it.

Another difference between a hobby and a business is that a business is supposed to make a profit; a hobby doesn't have to. In fact, if you set up a business and have not shown a profit after three years, the IRS may *declare* your business a hobby and disallow the business deductions you took for those three years. They don't always do this, though; they actually seem more concerned with enabling you to show that you are *trying* to make a profit.

Managing Money

When you do make a profit, what you do with it will go a long way toward determing whether or not you stay in business. Don has seen many dealers bring in some money on a good weekend and, instead of using it as operating capital, spend every penny of it on personal things. For example, you might have hauled a good chest and a corner cupboard to Myrtle Beach. Suppose you sold the chest to a dealer for $500, and the cupboard to another dealer for $1,000. There you are, at Myrtle Beach with $1,500 in your pocket. It feels like profit, so you think you've got it to spend. You spend an extra night in the motel, buy an expensive dinner, buy the kids bikes, get another television set, and pick up a video recorder. That about kills the $1,500. But the chest you sold originally cost you $400, and you paid $800 for the corner cupboard. The cost of those two pieces to you was $1,200, which means that of the $1,500 you had, only $300 was really profit. It seems so obvious that you may wonder why we bother to mention it. Unfortunately, no matter how obvious it seems in the abstract, there's something terribly seductive about money in your pocket. Unless you are religiously careful about separating personal and business expenditures, keeping records, and taking only real profit out of the business, the money will slip away and so will your business.

Bank Business

Business experts say you should establish separate bank accounts for your business and your personal life, even if you're only operating part-time, on a small scale. You should deposit all income of the business into the business account and pay only business expenses out of it. If you take out money for yourself, it should be noted and deposited into your personal account. This gives you a good record of your cash flow and simplifies bookkeeping.

Some banks charge more for handling business accounts than they do personal accounts. If they have interest-checking, some require a higher minimum balance to earn interest on a business account. Other banks give breaks to people opening business accounts. Shop around and find a bank that will be convenient and cooperative. The account you maintain as your business account does not have to be a business account from the bank's point of view, especially if you will be moving relatively small amounts of cash. Especially in the beginning, there's nothing to stop you from opening what the bank calls a personal account to use for your antiques business transactions.

Another bank service you may want to look into is establishing a line of credit. The antiques business is erratic. Money does not come and go predictably. Sometimes you may have an opportunity to make some good buys and find that you don't have the operating capital to do it because you bought heavily just a few days earlier and haven't yet sold what you bought. We've already said that if you keep too many things for yourself, your business will die because all your operating capital will be tied up in your living room, so to speak. But that's not what we are talking about now. We're assuming that you've made good, legitimate buys on salable goods that you just haven't had time to turn yet. A classic example would be if you'd been visited by a picker and made some very good purchases on Thursday. A few more things came in Friday. Saturday you go to an auction where attendance is poor, and you have a chance to pick up some great bargains. The trouble is you spent about all you had Thursday and Friday. You hate to lose the bargains just because your account is out of funds, when you know you'll be able to do some heavy selling in the coming week and build the account back up to operating level.

Generations of us have handled such problems on a personal and business level by kiting—writing checks we know aren't covered on the gamble that by the time the check clears we'll have been able to get money into the account to keep it from bouncing. It was never a good practice but you could usually get away with it. Now that banks are computerized, it often doesn't work. Checks clear too fast.

If you are already established with a bank and have a good credit rating, it shouldn't be difficult for you to arrange overdraft protection and a line of credit. Banks handle it in various ways, but overdraft protection simply means that the bank agrees not to bounce your checks without contacting you and giving you a chance to make them good first. At some banks you can arrange to have them automatically draw the necessary funds from your savings account or a specially arranged credit account. A line of credit means that you arrange with the bank for clearance to borrow money up to a set amount should you need it, but you don't actually take the money or pay interest on it until and unless you need it. None of these services are free. You'll pay interest on your loans and service fees on your overdrafts. But sometimes you may feel it is worth the expense to be able to take advantage of bargains you find.

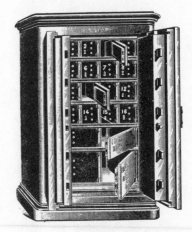

Setup and Maintenance

Now that we've gone over some of the general business considerations you will be involved with throughout the life of your business, we'll take you through the nitty-gritty steps of setting up and maintaining your business. We are concentrating mainly on those matters more or less unique to an antiques business. In the following chapter, on where to go for more help, we've listed several good books about how to run small businesses in general. You should read a couple of them for more amplification of basic small business principles.

Licenses and Permits

Your first step in getting yourself into the antiques business is to check on what licenses and permits you will need in your area. No federal licenses are needed. All licenses will be local. If you live in the country, you may not need anything but a permit to open a business. All Don had to get was a permanent $3 permit and a wholesale license. It could be more complicated if you live in a town with strict zoning or in a subdivision in which the properties have deed restrictions prohibiting business activities. To find out what you need in your area, check with the county courthouse and any homeowners' organizations that have jurisdiction over the property from which you plan to operate. Some places won't allow you to sell out of your house if your district is zoned residential. Of course, they can't do a thing about you loading a van and going to flea markets. If your plans include any new building to shelter your business, make sure you can get a building permit and can meet the local code requirements.

If your state has a sales tax, you will need a seller's permit of some sort and a state tax number. Some states also require a wholesale license if you will be selling to dealers. Call or write to the local state tax office for details because you almost certainly will sell to dealers sometimes, even if most of your business is retail.

Setting Up and Keeping Books

Have your bookkeeping system figured out before you ever see your first customer. You'll need it for recording the expenses of getting started. Besides, if you wait until you're in business, you may be tempted to put it off.

If you already have some sort of an accounting system that you like and understand, keep it. If you are starting from scratch, do it the simplest way you can. It's like people you've probably known who decide to take up skiing or tennis. The first thing they do is go out and buy the most elaborate equipment and clothing they can find. Then they head for the slopes or courts and try to figure out what to do with it. Don't start on a crash course in accounting. Don't spend a lot of money on big fancy ledgers or computer programs. Don started keeping his accounts in a school composition book. Ten years later, the same system is still working just fine, though he has graduated to two spiral notebooks.

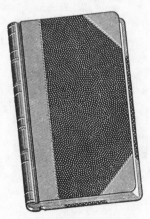

A Simple Accounting System

If you don't already have a system, here's what Don recommends. Keep a daily sales journal and a daily purchases journal. You can use two notebooks or write both sets of information on the same page of a daily diary or "daybook." Don carries a little pad in his pocket all the time to record transactions as soon as they're made. Each evening he transfers the information to his notebooks.

In the daily purchases journal, write down the date, what you bought (list each item), and the price you paid. If you bought an entire load, or box full, or lot, for one price, you should still break out each item and assign it a value so that the total of assigned values on all the items adds up to what you paid for the lot.

In the daily sales journal, write down the date, the items you sold, to whom, and for what price. You can keep track of sales using simple sales receipt books with carbons. They're sold in all office supply stores and even in many variety stores. As you write out each customer's receipt, you automatically make a record of the sale for yourself. But you still should transfer the information to a sales journal each day because the little receipt pads are easily lost. You may be using several different pads and lose track of one. Or you may leave it in your pocket and inadvertently run it through the washer and dryer.

As an additional double check at the end of each day, go back through your purchases journal marking off the items you've sold, noting price and date. This gives you a full history on each piece, including how much you made. At the end of the month it will be easy to run down the list and add up your month's earnings.

You'll also need an expenditures ledger or book in which to record all the other expenses of running your business. If you start small, these probably will be minimal, but you still need to keep track of such expenditures as postage, independent contractors' fees, hauling expenses, and business-related automobile expenses. If you pay by check, your checkbook serves as a record of the expenditures, but they still should be transferred to your expenses book and totalled every month.

When we began this book, IRS rules for auto mileage deductions required that you log the date, destination, beginning and ending odometer reading, total miles traveled, and purpose of travel for every trip. It was a colossal pain in the neck. A simplified procedure has been approved. If you use your vehicle only for business and you depreciate it, just keep a record of the odometer reading, date, and cost each time you buy gas. Also, keep receipts for all other automobile expenses. If you use your personal vehicle for some business, keep a trip diary for business. Record the date and number of miles of each trip. To be safe, note the purpose as well. You won't need gas purchase information because you'll be deducting business mileage from the total cost of operating your car. The best way to keep up with it is to keep a log book in your car and take the extra minute needed to write down all that information. Any driving you do related to your business, whether it's a trip to an auction or to the post office, qualifies as a business expense. It's worth the trouble it takes to write down the particulars because even short trips add up in a hurry, and without records you can't take the deductions. Why give the IRS anything you don't have to?

Inventory Records

The easiest way to keep track of what you have is to assign each piece an inventory or stock code. Use these codes on a sticker on each item to indicate the price you paid and the retail price you're charging. Assign each piece a stock number as you purchase it. Simply number what you buy in consecutive order. This allows you to find the items more easily later on in your purchases and inventory records. Some dealers like to keep information about what they paid for items private. To do this and still have the information at hand, they make up their stock codes by using a ten-letter word and translating the numbers into letters. For example, suppose you bought a sideboard for $75 and wanted to sell it for $300. It was purchase #1027. You've decided to base the purchase price in your code on the word "discourage." Here's how it would work:

$$\begin{array}{ccccccccccc} \text{D} & \text{I} & \text{S} & \text{C} & \text{O} & \text{U} & \text{R} & \text{A} & \text{G} & \text{E} \\ 0 & 1 & 2 & 3 & 4 & 5 & 6 & 7 & 8 & 9 \end{array}$$

$$\$75 = \text{AU}.$$

The stock code for that sideboard would be 1027 AU. The sticker on the item would read 1027 AU $300.

Now let's reverse the process. Suppose you have a walnut chest with this stock code on it: 2000 IRU $575. You can translate it to mean that the chest's stock number is 2000, its cost to you was $165, and its retail price is $575.

You can add numbers to the code to signify dates on which you bought pieces. If you had purchased two different sideboards for $70 each and were retailing both of them for $300 each, their *letter* code would be the same. But if you bought one on June 6 and the other on July 1, the sequential stock number would tell you which came first. Date numbers would be even more specific.

Some canny shoppers enjoy figuring out your codes and knowing what you paid for things. When you've made a fairly normal markup, it doesn't really matter. If you've hit a lick, you might prefer that a customer not know that the antique with a retail price of $500 came to you for $40. To make your code a little more secret, you might reverse the order of the wholesale and retail prices or put the number for the month at the beginning and the number for the day at the end of the letter group. Almost any simple permutation would be enough. Most customers aren't cryptologists.

If you have very high and rapid turnover, as Don does, you may not be able to keep up with such coding. Its greatest advantage is in a shop where business is mainly retail. It keeps full information about each piece right at your fingertips and is especially useful if someone else also sells for you in the shop. It simplifies writing down the sale in the sales journal. Another advantage of the code is that it allows you to distinguish quickly between similar objects.

Even if you don't bother with stock codes or numbers, your purchases journal serves as a complete record of your inventory. That's why it's important to remember to mark off each item you sell. At least once a year, you should check your actual stock against your inventory records. You may catch anything from theft to mistakes in your records while making sure that your inventory map accurately reflects the stock territory. Seeing, on paper, what has been selling well and what has been moving slowly may guide your future buying. Also, you'll need the information about your stock for figuring taxes.

Taxes

Unless you are experienced in figuring taxes for a business, you should have some help from an accountant at least the first year. And it's a good idea to consult the accountant as you are setting up, to be sure you have all the necessary information in a usable form at tax time. State and county taxes on businesses vary widely. Federal law requires you to keep a record of sales for tax purposes. You'll have this if you keep your sales journal faithfully.

Of course, you expect to pay federal income tax. If you haven't been self-employed before, you may not be prepared to pay self-employment taxes, which is the government's way of getting Social Security taxes out of you when there's no employer withholding them. And *you* have to pay the whole amount, whereas you had to pay only half when you worked for someone else. If you still work for someone else part of the time and Social Security taxes are being withheld, it will probably reduce considerably the amount of self-employment tax you must pay.

When you are self-employed and have no other employer, you have to pay your income tax quarterly, in advance, since it can't be withheld from regular salary checks. The hard part, in the beginning, is estimating accurately the amount of money you'll be earning and the corresponding amount of taxes you owe. If you get the estimate too far wrong, you have to pay a penalty. Fortunately, you can revise your estimates during the year.

Beyond that, you may have to contend with a states sales tax on retail sales, and in most states a state income tax. Some counties have property taxes that would include the inventory of your business. You may have to do a monthly state sales tax report. Your local tax office will have the pertinent details. It's crucial to have all this information and understand it before you begin in business, because, inevitably, you'll end up paying more taxes if you have poor records. It is usually worth the money to have the help of an accountant the first time around.

The good news is that if your state has a sales tax, your seller's permit (which requires you to collect tax and pass it on to the state) will allow you to buy goods for resale (wholesale) without paying taxes on them.

Probably you'll be working both sides of the street as far as the tax advantage in wholesale activity goes. You'll be selling some things wholesale to other dealers (which is why you need the wholesale permit we mentioned above), and you'll be buying some things wholesale *from* other dealers for resale (which is why you need the seller's permit). You won't pay sales tax on either transaction.

Insurance

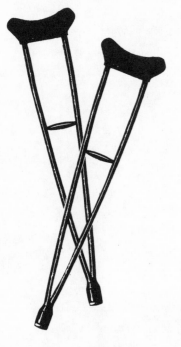

The trouble with insurance is that the more you need it, the harder it is to get and the more it costs. If you have customers coming to your place of business, you should have liability insurance. It isn't hard to get unless your place is a death trap. If you keep inventory, you should have fire and theft coverage. And if you operate out of a big, rattling shed or barn, hard to lock but easy to burn and easy to get hurt in, you're going to find insurance companies less than eager to do business with you. They may have specific requirements about locks and alarms. If you have tanks of stripper on the premises, you may have to meet special fire-prevention measures such as keeping the stripper in a separate building before you can get insurance. To reduce their risk, some dealers have actually given up retail selling and become strictly wholesale because of the problems of getting liability insurance, though as one cynic has observed, "How much liability you need depends on what you're worth. If you don't own anything, a person suing you can't get what ain't there."

The important thing to remember is that not all insurance companies are alike. You may find rates for the coverage you need exorbitant with one company and tolerably reasonable with another. The policies they offer may range from covering only the building and not its contents to insuring all merchandise including what's in your vehicle when you haul it. As a general principle, insurance companies prefer to insure the kinds of business operations with which they're familiar, where they understand the risks. When they encounter an unfamiliar situation, they deal with it by making the cost of insuring high. When an insurance company must decide about an unusual situation, they usually follow the recommendations of the local agent who is setting up the policy. No company specializes in insuring antiques dealers, but your best deal probably will come from a company with agents doing business with other people in the antiques business. What you really need is a brother-in-law who is an insurance agent and thinks you're wonderful. Short of that, shop around before you commit.

Employees

Don't have any. As a beginner, the cost and requisite bureaucracy of having official employees will do you in. For instance, you'll have to keep payroll records for each person you employ. You'll have to withhold federal income tax, pay half their Social Security tax and withhold the other half. You'll have to withhold state income tax. You'll have to pay unemployment taxes and worker's compensation insurance premiums. If you have a Keough retirement plan for yourself, you'll have to pay into it for them, too. And you'll have to contend with all the attendant paperwork. This applies whether the employees are full- or part-time.

According to the IRS, an employee is anyone who "performs services that can be controlled by an employer." If you provide the materials and workplace, you're an employer.

When you need help, hire an independent contractor to do what you need done. For instance, instead of employing someone part-time to come into your shop and refinish furniture for an hourly wage, have someone finish pieces at home for you and invoice you for the job. (Even this is not completely trouble-free. If you pay an independent contractor $600 or more a year, you have to file a federal form with the IRS showing the contractor's name, address, Social Security number, and the amount you paid. The contractor also has to receive a copy of the form.)

Getting jobs such as refinishing and hauling done by independent contractors is a fairly straightforward matter. If you find you need an extra clerk in your shop, however, you're probably going to have to become an employer eventually. When you do, work with your accountant to make sure you have everything set up properly. But be aware that when you officially add an employee, your paperwork and expenses will about triple. If you can manage by hiring an occasional helper, much as you would a babysitter, or by confining your shop hours to what you can manage alone, or by using a little help from friends and family, do it that way for as long as possible. That way you'll at least have a running start before you get into the morass of being an employer.

Kinds of Business Arrangements

When you start thinking about needing help, you may be tempted to consider going into partnership with another person to begin your business. Don feels so strongly against partnerships in the antiques business that he would go to any lengths to avoid it. Most of the small businesses in this country, including antiques businesses, are sole proprietorships. They are easiest to start and easiest to run. In a sole proprietorship, there is no legal distinction between you and your business. If your business goes into debt, you are in debt. If your business is sued, you are sued. But you are in charge, and if you make any money, it's yours.

Partnerships also make no legal distinction between the partners and the business. If the business is in debt, the partners are in debt. But here's the bad part. The law doesn't distinguish between partners, either. If one of you does something dumb or something illegal, you're both responsible. If your partner flips a cork and writes $6,000 worth of bad checks for the business and then disappears, you're liable for the money. Add to that the inevitable difficulties of getting along with a spouse or friend once you've taken the burdens of a business upon yourselves, and you can see how easily such a venture could be the end of a friendship or marriage and the end of the business, too.

Don says that if he had to go into business with someone, he would incorporate before he would consider a partnership. Incorporating has many headaches, too. One of the greatest is paperwork. And, to avoid being taxed twice — once on the corporate income and once on the salary your corporation pays you — you must file a Sub S report at a given time and in very specific ways. It's a lot of work with an added time pressure, because if you miss the date by even a day, you'll end up paying heavy penalties. There are a lot of niggling little rules involved in corporations, especially in the Sub S, and it costs money if you fail to follow them exactly. It's true that you're not liable personally for the corporation's debts, but if you are beginning in business and not well known to the bank, you'll probably have to take any loans in your own name anyhow.

At least until you are established, the traditional sole proprietorship is the least troublesome and least costly way to go. Then you and your business are one. You're in charge.

Managing Overhead

We saved the problems of overhead until last; we might well have treated them first. Certainly we've been alluding to them all along. Quite simply, if you don't control overhead, the cost of doing business will put you out of business. For people with a taste for the good life, an inclination always to go first class, and a determination to own only the best of everything, overhead is going to be a challenge.

Although there are some notable exceptions, antiques businesses tend to range from marginal to modest. The difference between making it and not lies in never spending a penny to operate that you don't have to spend. Don's business stands as an outstanding example of costs kept to an absolute minimum.

We'll start by acknowledging the one area where Don doesn't control spending as tightly as he might — paying pickers and other people who wholesale antiques to him. We said in the chapter on buying that Don sometimes buys loads he doesn't really want because he knows the seller needs money. Don sometimes pays more than he thinks he should for items because he wants to give his pickers as good a break as he can. Don can make a pretty good case for the notion that what he spends in paying people eventually comes back to him in loyalty, favors, and opportunities to buy that he wouldn't otherwise enjoy.

But in the other areas of overhead, Don scores points for economy.

Location. If you have to pay rent on a shop, it's a fixed monthly expense. You can't start thinking about profits until you've sold enough to meet that monthly expense. Don's shop is on the family farm. He uses buildings that otherwise would stand empty.

Telephone. Don's parents tolerate his use of their phone and extensions for shop business. Another fixed monthly payment avoided.

Heat, light, air conditioning. Well, you open the doors at both ends of the barns and the breezes blow through. That's free air conditioning all summer. In the winter only one building is heated and that's done with a woodstove Don picked up for a few dollars years ago. It's fueled with wood cut on the property. As for light, we're not going to claim that all six barns are lighted with a single 25-watt bulb, but you definitely won't find banks of bright lights everywhere, and when nobody's in a building, the juice is off.

Transportation. We told you about that old farm truck that has hauled more thousands of dollars' worth of antiques than most shiny vans or high-power pickups. It was paid for long ago. Current costs are only for insurance, repairs, and gas.

Advertising. Business cards. A sign out front. An occasional small ad in a regional antiques periodical. Nothing more is really needed because most of Don's business comes from repeat customers, and word-of-mouth brings in new people. (Advertising is more critical for new dealers looking for customers, but going to flea markets, and being active buying and selling is the best way to become known.)

Office equipment. Don keeps his books on spiral notebooks, which are a lot cheaper than fancy ledgers. He has a calculator. His business doesn't require much in the way of correspondence, but if it did, he'd probably type the letters on the same Oliver typewriter his father used to type his college papers.

You can see that there's no glamour in Don's setup. He talks about eventually building a more elaborate showroom, but he has avoided the temptation to sink operating capital into an expensive building or furnishings or even a shiny sign for his truck. He prefers to put all he can into inventory that he can sell. Inventory can earn money; overhead can't.

Don believes you need to control the fixed monthly expenses in the rest of your life, too, if you're going to keep a fledgling antiques business prospering. After all, if you are a sole proprietorship, you

and your business are one. Whatever you can save in your personal life is money you don't have to take out of your business for personal expenses.

Don is proud of the fact that he is able to "live out of my junk" as much as he does. He hates malls and he hates to buy anything he can get some other way. His good dress suit came to him when he bought out a store in a deal that included some old, old clothing. The suit fits him perfectly, even though he's tall and skinny. He thinks it was probably left in the store's stock only because few tall skinny customers came looking for suits. The suit is better made than anything you could buy today and, for the moment at least, it's back in style. As for the rest of his wardrobe, everything from his sweater to his britches has a story and you can bet he didn't buy any of it directly.

Of course, he has collected much of what he uses in his home over years of buying loads. And the car he drives when he isn't hauling antiques is a little red Honda.

All this is appropriate to Don's personal values and the kind of business he operates. You might have to make some changes if you wanted a business that specialized in something other than rough country pieces and buying and selling by the truckload. But the underlying principles don't change. You should resist the impulse to get expensive equipment that you're tempted to buy solely because you happen to like office equipment. Don has noticed that the people who start out with big new trucks and fancy high-priced equipment usually don't last very long.

Looking at a computer? Computer advertising has made it sound as though anybody who doesn't have one has already been left behind in another century. It's true that you can buy computer programs for business that do everything but get up and walk around with you. But will you be operating on a scale where it can do more for you *that matters* than you can manage with a couple of pencils and a worksheet? In the beginning, you don't have to have a computer any more than you have to have a cash register. Lots of people have done lots of business well without either one. When the computer breaks, you'll end up with pencils and paper anyway.

Quality letterhead is nice. It's expensive. How many letters would you have to write to use it up? Will those letters net you more on expensive letterhead than they would typed on plain bond?

Anytime you are thinking of spending money for something besides inventory in your business, the questions in your mind should be, "How much more will I have to sell to pay for this?" and "How will this improve my business and how long will it take to do it?"

Does it all sound too Spartan? Were you hoping to live like the rich folks live? It reminds us of an old "Candid Camera" television show. The setup was a penny dropped in a conspicuous place on the sidewalk to see who would bother to bend over and pick it up. A number of people who looked like they could have used some money ignored the penny and walked on by. It was an obviously well-to-do woman in a fur coat who finally took it, and she dirtied her white gloves picking up the penny.

If you don't love antiques and buying and selling and all the quirks that go into the business well enough to pick up the pennies, you'll find controlling overhead and personal expenses a hardship. But if you're the kind of person who loves the business so much that work is more fun than play would be, and if your idea of a good time has something to do with finding, buying, or selling some more antiques, you won't think in terms of an austerity program. You'll just think about how lucky you are to have something to do that you'd rather be spending time on than anything else in the world.

CHAPTER 8

Where to Go for More Help

It's bound to happen. After you read this book, you're going to start thinking of questions that we haven't dealt with. And as you take your first steps toward setting up your business, you're going to want more detail about something — antiques or business practices or the psychology of customers. In this chapter we offer you a wealth of places to go for more help. Being avid readers, we have many suggestions for books and periodicals. In addition to what we have here, you should read everything you can find about any areas in which you specialize. Along with your reading, you'll find in-the-flesh resources are helpful, too.

Other Dealers and Collectors

People already in antiques can give you more help than you'll get from any other source. It's true that some dealers will see you as a competitor and be thoroughly obnoxious, but most antiques dealers are genuinely nice people. Dealers hang around together and realize that they need each other. And they love to talk shop. Let it be known that you're thinking of getting into the business and describe your specialty. You'll probably get more advice than you know what to do with. Some of it will contradict ours. As a guide to knowing whose advice to follow and whose to ignore beyond your own instinctive reactions to people, we'd say trust those who are making a go of it.

Collectors can be useful to you not only as potential customers, but also as a source of insight into the collector's mentality and as contacts with other potential buyers and sellers.

Other People With Small Businesses

At first glance, you may not see many similarities between a restaurant and a service station and an antiques business, but to the degree that all succeed by adhering to sound and good business practices, they are alike. Talk to people who have successful businesses. Tell them what you have in mind, and in evaluating their responses just mentally allow for the ways you know working in antiques differs from food service or garage jobs.

Small Business Development

Some states offer free advice to people thinking about going into business for themselves. The offices often are run as part of a business adminstration curriculum at a state college or university.

Business students work as consultants in the offices just as education students practice student teaching in the classroom. Nobody in such an office is likely to have any advice about antiques, but you may find some useful hand-holding in business matters such as taxes and bookkeeping, location, financing, and advertising. For a free directory of small business development offices, write: SBA Office of Advocacy, 1726 I Street, NW, Room 408, Washington, D.C. 20416. Ask for *The States and Small Businesses: Programs and Activities*. Also, a call to the largest educational institution in your area will put you on to such resources.

Community College and Adult Education Courses

Virtually all colleges and universities are looking for ways to expand their student base now that the baby boomers are past college age. Life-long education programs abound. You can find courses lasting anywhere from half a day to half a year in personal finance, business, accounting, marketing, psychology, interpersonal communication, and a plethora of other areas related to running a business. Some of them are useful; some of them are dreadful. Word-of-mouth will tell you more than the school's publicity. A tired secretary associated with the program may tell you even more late on a Friday afternoon. So will people who have already taken the class in earlier sessions. Sometimes you can get a feel for how useful a course would be by contacting the instructor and chatting briefly. Maybe you can save time and money by reading the books used in the courses and skipping the actual classes.

Classes in refinishing, woodworking, chair caning, and studies of antiques are offered by local institutions, too. If you are interested in the skills they teach, it would probably be worth taking the class, but Don has observed that the people associated with classes related to antiques rarely have much to say about making a buck, so you'd get knowledge of antiques but not of the antiques *business* from such classes.

Reading Material on the Subject

Periodicals

Useful periodicals fall into two categories: general interest and decorator magazines whose content will give you clues to developing fads and tastes; and publications specifically about antiques. Our list is by no means exhaustive, but we've included those we know are most widely read. Some are for dealers and consumers; some are trade journals just for dealers.

General publications on homes and decorating. Published six times a year by Special Interest Publications is *Traditional Home* (Publishing Group of Meredith Corporation, 1716 Locust Street, Des Moines, Iowa 50336). This slick magazine increasingly is emphasizing the use of antiques in today's homes. It deals also with reproductions, building materials, and collecting. Of course, it is packed with pictures of redecorated rooms, many of them incorporating historic patterns in fabric and wallpaper. The magazine includes a useful section on "Information Worth Writing For," a lengthy list of booklets and other publications about everything from how to finish wood moldings to the consumer's guide to oil heating. These booklets are free from manufacturers.

Country Living, published monthly by the Hearst Corporation, 224 West 57th Avenue, New York, New York 10019. If you wonder about a "country" magazine being published in the city, you may find reassurance in knowing that the staff come from all over the place and travel a lot to stay in touch with their area of expertise. The magazine publishes articles and photographs about living "country style." They're especially interested in country furniture, pottery, quilts, and information about antiques generally. When they feature a particular kind of antique, such as country folk art painted pieces, there's an immediate corresponding wave of customers in antiques shops and flea markets looking for the kinds of pieces featured.

Don says *Country Living* probably has done more to build up the current nationwide interest in the country look and country antiques than any other publication. (Amusingly enough, they somehow manage to mix articles about early American bedrooms and primitive furniture with ads for Tupperware and make it all fit.)

House Beautiful, published monthly by the Hearst Corporation, 1700 Broadway, New York, New York 10019. The emphasis here is more on design, architecture, and building than on furnishings, but many issues deal with historical subjects, including restorations; antiques show up frequently in the rooms photographed.

Southern Living, published monthly by Southern Living, Inc., 820 Shades Creek Parkway, Birmingham, Alabama 35209. You almost have to see this magazine to understand it; it defies adequate description. The editorial content is unrelentingly Southern, which means emphasis on the way things used to be — old-style gardens, homes, furnishings, and recipes. One gets the feeling that everybody in the South reads it; its influence is undeniable.

Sunset Magazine, published monthly by Lane Publishing Company, Willow and Middlefield Roads, Menlo Park, California 94025. This is another of those almost overwhelming life-style magazines, emphasizing travel, building, food, and gardening. The magazine's approach to antiques reflects the fact that they are harder to find and more expensive on the West Coast. It, too, is influential, and you can count on a feature article on a subject such as native American art or Pueblo rugs to send readers out to the antiques shops looking for same.

Yankee, published monthly by Yankee Publishing Corporation, Dublin, New Hampshire 03444. All the articles in this small-format magazine have a New England slant. Emphasis is on history, arts, crafts, and antiques to look for.

Antiques periodicals. The most important publication for collectors and dealers in antiques and collectibles is *The Antique Trader Weekly* (Box 1050, Dubuque, Iowa 52001). If you want to sound knowledgeable, call it "The Trader." It's a weekly newspaper that carries articles on all types of antiques and collectors' items, as well as in-depth stories about new shops. Recently, a dealer observed that it seemed to contain more ads than articles, but even so, it's the single most useful source of information for customers and dealers about what's going on in the business.

Antique Monthly, published by Boone, Inc., P.O. Drawer 2, Tuscaloosa, Alabama 35401. This is a monthly tabloid with many articles and ads and a national readership — another good publication for keeping up with what's going on in the business.

Antiques Dealer, 1115 Clifton Avenue, Clifton, New Jersey 07013. You have to show letterhead or business cards to prove that you're really a professional in the business before you can even subscribe to this trade journal. It's the only strictly *trade* journal in the antiques business. It features current events related to the antiques business, business news, auctions news, and a dealer-of-the-month profile. The international antiques shows calendar in the back of each issue is especially interesting. Useful for learning how dealers think.

Antiques Journal, published by Babka Publishing Company, Inc., Box 1046, Dubuque, Iowa 52001. This is *The Antique Trader Weekly's* monthly magazine. It carries articles on antiques and collectibles and, like *The Trader,* lots of ads.

Antiques Magazine, 551 Fifth Avenue, New York, New York 10176. This slick monthly is expensive to subscribe to and features mostly upscale antiques, including European pieces, fine art, and porcelain. Definitely the publication to check if you've always wondered what a $5,000 chair looks like.

Kovels' on Antiques and Collectibles, edited and published by Ralph and Terry Kovel, Box 222000, North Beachwood, Ohio 44122. A monthly newsletter of tips and information for buying and selling antiques.

Schroeder's Insider & Price Update, published by Collector Books, P.O. Box 3009, Paducah, Kentucky 42001. A sixteen-page monthly newsletter that is newer on the scene than *Kovels'.* Probably the best way to tell if it would be useful or not is to look at several issues.

Books About Antiques

The books we suggest here scarcely represent even a fraction of those available. We have limited our suggestions to those that seem especially appropriate for beginners, but as you become increasingly knowledgeable, you will find many more books that you will want to add to your professional library.

How to Make Easy Money in Antiques, by Dan Shiaras, published by Collector Books, P.O. Box 3009, Paducah, Kentucky 42001, 1984. This is not a book we agree with, but you need to know about it anyhow. Publicity for the book says that Shiaras has been dealing with antiques for fifty years. He was in advertising. His writing and his advice are about what you'd expect from an ad man who got into antiques. He talks a lot about gaining psychological advantages, spending big, and hitting the big licks. Definitely a contrast to our advice, but a pretty clear exposition of the other side.

How to Make Money in the Antiques-and-Collectibles Business, by Elyse Sommer, published by Houghton Mifflin Company, Boston, 1979. Sommer's book differs substantially from Shiaras' in tone and content. She's not suggesting that there's anything easy about the business. And she's given more sober thought to down-to-earth business considerations. Sommer is basically a crafts and hobby writer. Her book differs from ours in that it relies on the examples of other dealers, rather than on firsthand experience for its advice. Sommer writes about some antiques-related job possibilities, such as writing and mail order, that you may find useful.

Kovels' Antiques and Collectibles Price List, 17th ed., edited by Ralph and Terry Kovel, published by Crown Publishers, Inc., 1 Park Avenue, New York, New York 10016. A standard reference of 45,000 listings, printed from a computer print-out.

Schroeder's Antiques Price Guide, edited by Sharon and Bob Huxford, published by Collector Books, P.O. Box 3009, Paducah, Kentucky 42001. For beginners, here is a useful and overwhelming book. It lists more than 58,000 antiques and collectibles and their approximate retail prices. Of course, it doesn't help you understand fluctuating values affected by location and current fads, and if you already have specialties, you'll notice that listings are far from complete. But it's a wonderful book to get started with and a standard reference when you're in unfamiliar territory any time. Don prefers this to the Kovels' price guide, which is printed from a computer print-out. Schroeder's is organized alphabetically by subject, making it easy to find what you want.

The Sears and Roebuck Catalogs, reproductions, published by Nostalgia Books, distributed by Crown Publishers, Inc., 1 Park Avenue, New York, New York 10016. We're not kidding. Old catalogs give you the clearest descriptions you can find anywhere of every piece of merchandise they sold, along with pictures. The old-timey prices will make you sigh, but they'll be useful in helping you figure current values. Some of the original old catalogs are still around, but they're expensive collectors' items now. Even if you found any, you'd probably prefer to have the repros for day-to-day study so that you wouldn't wear out the originals.

Montgomery Ward Catalogs, Dover Publications, Inc., 11 East 2nd Street, Mineola, New York 11501. These catalogs are equally useful.

Books About Business

Small Time Operator: How to Start Your Own Small Business, Keep Your Books, Pay Your Taxes, and Stay Out of Trouble, A Guide and Workbook, by Bernard Kamoroff, C.P.A., Bell Springs Publishing, Box 640, Laytonville, California 95454, 1984. Kamoroff's book, now in its nineteenth printing, probably shows up in the bibliographies and resources chapters of more books for artists, writers, photographers, freelancers, and other people planning to go independent than any other business book. Well it should. Kamoroff's book truly lives up to its title. Moreover, it's all written so that nonbusiness types can understand. For $1 and a self-addressed, stamped envelope, Kamoroff will send you an update sheet listing changes in tax laws and other government regulations every January. He calls his book a workbook because in the back it contains a year's worth of blank ledger sheets for expenditures, income, and credit transactions.

Straight Talk About Small Business, by Kenneth J. Albert, published by McGraw Hill, 1221 Avenue of the Americas, New York, New York 10020, 1981. Bernard Kamoroff, the author of *Small Time Operator,* recommends this book because it covers areas he hasn't covered — selling, the market, ways of getting a business started, the skills it takes, and the problems you may have. It is very useful for helping to keep your mind set in a business-oriented direction.

Offerings From the Bureaucracy

The Internal Revenue Service offers a series of good booklets that are useful for anyone opening up an antiques business, or any other small business, for that matter.

> *Tax Guide for Small Businesses* #334
> *Tax Withholding and Declaration of Estimated Tax* #505
> *Information on Self-Employment Tax* #533
> *Tax Information on Business Expenses* #535
> *Tax Information on Self-Employed Retirement Plans* #560
> *Record Keeping for a Small Business* #583

Call your local IRS office to find out how to get these booklets, or write: Internal Revenue Service, United States Government Printing Office, Washington, D.C. 20402.

These guides are all either free or very inexpensive. Maybe it's an apology for all the grief that taxes give us.

The Small Business Administration also offers many free and inexpensive booklets. Those you might find especially useful include *Starting and Managing a Small Business* and *Staffing Your Store.* However, many other publications are available, and you should request lists. To get the booklets, you can either call the nearest SBA office, which will be listed in the Federal Government section of your telephone directory, or write: Small Business Administration, Box 15434, Fort Worth, Texas 76119.

Fun Reading

You'll be amazed at how much you can learn about antiques and how fun you can have doing it by digging out old magazines at the library and studying the advertisements. You'll probably get sucked into reading the stories and articles, too. As you turn the pages, you find yourself putting together a sense of what life was like at the time the magazine was published. Even if you read issues published during your adult lifetime, you'll be surprised at how much you can learn and how nostalgic it makes you feel. Magazine ads can tell you when frozen orange juice was introduced, when typewriters began to have standard keyboards, what the first electric washing machines looked like and, most fascinating of all, how people reacted to all these newfangled inventions. This kind of reading is just plain fun, and it generates a sense of the significance of antiques you can't get any other way.

Finally, we'd like to recommend the novels of Jonathan Gash, published by St. Martin's Press. They are suspense stories about the world of antiques in England. The hero, or nonhero more accurately, is Lovejoy, an antiques dealer who is always broke, always in trouble, and thinks antiques are more important than anything or anybody. He's a "natural divey," a person born with the ability to divine authentic antiques and spot fakes. The novels are quick and fun to read. They ease you into the language of the business as it is practiced in England and give you wonderful glimpses of the great variety of characters who inhabit the rather peculiar world of antiques here and abroad. Along the way, they'll teach you something about antiques. Two titles to start with are *The Gondola Scam* and *Firefly Gadroon*.

Maybe we're making a mistake to conclude with suggestions for pleasure reading. Maybe after reading this book you'll skip right into the fiction, without ever getting around to the *doing* of your business at all. We hope not. Because starting your own antiques business in one of the ways we've described is completely possible, and it would be a pure shame to stop with reading about it.

And we'd hate for you to miss out on the satisfaction and fun — and sometimes even money — that comes with being in the business. Think about the 90-year-old man who is still buying and selling truckloads of antiques. The only rocking chairs he cares about are those he can trade for profit. Think about all the specialists who have an extra reason for visiting shops to pick up and sell goodies when they travel. Think about becoming an insider in the antiques business instead of just a customer.

If dealing in antiques has been a dream of yours, you're lucky. This is one of the few businesses we know in which you can bring the dream to life with practically no risk, by starting small. Isn't it great that the antiques business is so well suited to starting with a little and growing into a lot?

Do read everything you can find, including what we've suggested, about being in antiques. But don't stop there. Put down the books, climb out of the chair (even if it is an antique) and *go for it!*

Good luck and great fun!

A

Accounting, 78, 81–82, 85
Adult education courses, 92
Advertising, 15, 24, 51, 57
Antique auctions, 28–29
Antique Monthly, 94
The Antique Trader Weekly, 17, 94
Antiques Dealer, 94
Antiques Journal, 94
Antiques Magazine, 94
Appraisals, 52
"Auction fever," 34–35
"Auction finish," 34
Auction houses, 27–28
"Auction merchandise," 33–34
Auctioneers, 29, 30, 31, 36–37, 38–39, 41–42
Auctions, 27–42; antique, 28–29; bidding at, 34, 35, 36, 37, 38–40; dealers at, 35–36; estate, 28, 40–41; how to act at, 30–36; how they work, 36–42; junk, 30; prices at, 27, 28, 40
Auto mileage deductions, 81–82

B

Bank business, 78–79
Bankruptcy sales, 29
Bargaining, 50–51, 52–54, 69–70
Bidding, 34, 35, 36, 37, 38–40
Bookkeeping, 77–78, 80–84
Books, 94–96
Browsing, 58, 59
Business arrangements, 85–86
Business bank accounts, 78–79
Business cards, 19, 62
Business practice, 77–89
Buying, 43–56; for customers, 53, 58–59; instincts, 46–50; moving sales, 51–52; negotiating prices, 50–51, 52–54; out of homes, 51–52; from suppliers, 54–56; time factor, 48–49; yard sales, 50–51

C

Capital, operating, 13
Carolina Antique News, 17

Cash accounting, 78
Chairs, 33–34
Checks, 73–74, 79
China, 33
Classes on business- and antique-related subjects, 92
Classified advertisements, 15, 24, 51
Cleaning pieces, 21–22
Coins, 12
Collectibles, 53
Collectors, 53, 71, 91
Commission, 20
Consignment, 11, 21
Counter offers, 53
Country antiques, 48
Country auctions, 28–29
Country Living, 47, 93
Credit, 74, 79
Curly maple furniture, 12
Customer relations, 16, 73–76
Customers, 53, 57–61, 62–64

D

"Dead man's sales," 28
Dealer auctions, 28–29
Dealers, 1–7, 35–36, 71, 91
Dealer's going-out-of-business sales, 29–30
Decisions, early, 11–12
Display, 21–22, 65–67
Door knocking, 22–25

E

Empire furniture, 48
Employees, 85
Estate auctions, 28, 40–41
Estimating the market, 45–46
Ethics, 22, 24
Expenditures ledger, 81

F

Fads, 46–48, 49
Firearms, 12
Five basic rules for buying at auctions, 31–36
Flea markets, 17–19, 67–68
Folk art, 46–47
Furniture display, 67

G

Gash, Jonathan: *Firefly Gadroon,* 97; *The Gondola Scam,* 97
Glass, 33
Gold, 12
Guns, 12

H

Haggling, 50–51, 52–54, 69–70
Haulers, 38
Homes: buying out of, 51–52; selling from, 20–21
House Beautiful, 93
How to Make Easy Money in Antiques, 95
How to Make Money in the Antiques-and-Collectibles Business, 95

I

Independent contractors, 85
Incorporating, 86
Information on Self-Employment Tax, 96
Instincts, 49–50
Insurance, 84
Internal Revenue Service, 55, 78, 81-82, 85, 96
Inventory records, 16, 82–83

J

Jewelry, expensive, 12
Junk auctions, 30

K

"Keepitis," 6, 70–72
Kiting checks, 79
"Knock-out bidding," 39
Kovels' Antiques and Collectibles Price List, 95

L

Layaway, 74–75
License plates, 47–48
Licenses for business, 80
Low bids, 38

Other Books of Interest

How to Find and Buy Your Business in the Country. Shows you, step-by-step, how to evaluate a business, assess your finances, make an offer, get organized, and run a country business successfully. $11.95, paperback. Order #373-9.

How to Run A Country Store. Here are all the particulars for those interested in country stores: how to determine a fair price for the business, what inventory to carry, what changes (if any) to make, how to determine your customers' needs, promotion ideas, bookkeeping, and more! $9.95, paperback. Order #397-6.

Country Wisdom Bulletins

Braiding Rugs. How to create easy-to-make rugs using either new or old materials. The finished product will look great in any room, will be reversible, and is easily cleaned. $1.95 each. Order Bulletin #A-3.

Chair Caning. Breath new life into an old and broken chair seat. All you need are simple tools from around the home, inexpensive materials, and this bulletin. The results will give you great satisfaction. $1.95 each. Order Bulletin #A-16.

Refinishing Pine Furniture. Even the worst-looking furniture can be transformed into attractive pieces. Here's what's included: the time you will need, tools, how to handle paint removers, stains, and varnishes. $1.95 each. Order Bulletin #A-31.

Making Baskets. An instructor, and long-time basket-making enthusiast, shows you how to do it for yourself. You'll be ready then to try new ideas and different materials. Basket-making is a wonderful hobby, and a marketable craft and gift endeavor. $1.95 each. Order Bulletin #A-96.

Please add $2.50 to your order for postage and handling ($4.00 for UPS). Send orders to: Garden Way Publishing, Dept. 8900, Schoolhouse Road, Pownal, VT 05261.

Write for our free catalog.